What Life Was Like®

IN THE REALM OF ELIZABETH

England
AD 1533 ~ 1603

What Life Was Like

IN THE REALM OF ELIZABETH

England
AD 1533 – 1603

BY THE EDITORS OF TIME-LIFE BOOKS, ALEXANDRIA, VIRGINIA

CONTENTS

In the Realm of Elizabeth

Reformation, Rebellion, and War

When Elizabeth I ascended the throne in 1558 at the age of 25, England was a kingdom in jeopardy, ravaged by religious turmoil and costly conflicts with France and Scotland. Many Englishmen feared that Elizabeth could never provide the strong and steady leadership they needed without a husband to guide her. She would prove them wrong.

Elizabeth belonged to the Tudor dynasty, founded in 1485 by her grandfather, Henry VII. Her father, Henry VIII, strengthened the Crown but also squandered a fortune on foreign conflicts and unsettled his realm by rejecting papal authority. He fathered three successors by different wives: Edward VI, who furthered the English reformation to the dismay of the nation's Catholics; Mary I, who antagonized Protestants by restoring Rome's authority and marrying Philip of Spain, heir to the throne of that mighty Catholic power; and Elizabeth I, who sought to stabilize her country by establishing a moderate form of Protestantism and concluding peace with France and Scotland.

Peace at home was shattered in 1568 with the arrival of Elizabeth's Catholic cousin Mary Stuart, who had been forced to abdicate the Scottish throne. Knowing that many English Catholics wanted Mary as their queen, Elizabeth put her under house arrest. A

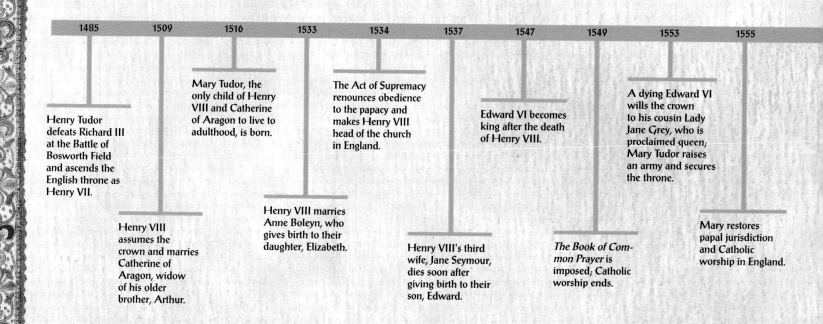

1485 — Henry Tudor defeats Richard III at the Battle of Bosworth Field and ascends the English throne as Henry VII.

1509 — Henry VIII assumes the crown and marries Catherine of Aragon, widow of his older brother, Arthur.

1516 — Mary Tudor, the only child of Henry VIII and Catherine of Aragon to live to adulthood, is born.

1533 — Henry VIII marries Anne Boleyn, who gives birth to their daughter, Elizabeth.

1534 — The Act of Supremacy renounces obedience to the papacy and makes Henry VIII head of the church in England.

1537 — Henry VIII's third wife, Jane Seymour, dies soon after giving birth to their son, Edward.

1547 — Edward VI becomes king after the death of Henry VIII.

1549 — The Book of Common Prayer is imposed; Catholic worship ends.

1553 — A dying Edward VI wills the crown to his cousin Lady Jane Grey, who is proclaimed queen; Mary Tudor raises an army and secures the throne.

1555 — Mary restores papal jurisdiction and Catholic worship in England.

rebellion aimed at installing Mary as England's ruler broke out in the north, but Elizabeth's troops quickly stemmed the revolt.

Aside from that rebellion and brief interventions on behalf of Protestants in Scotland and France, England remained at peace from 1558 until the mid-1580s, and the nation grew stronger at home and abroad. London boomed as thousands flocked from around the country to a city ripe with opportunities for rogues and reformers, doctors and lawyers, playwrights and pamphleteers. In this age of enterprise, merchants and the Crown supported adventurers like Sir Francis Drake and Sir Walter Raleigh in their efforts to explore and colonize distant lands—and plunder Spanish treasure ships.

The conflict with Spain intensified in 1585 when Elizabeth sent troops to aid breakaway Protestant provinces of the northern Netherlands against their Spanish overlords. Spain,

meanwhile, was encouraging rebellious English Catholics in their efforts to depose Elizabeth in favor of Mary—whose involvement in one such plot led to her execution in 1587. The following year, English forces handed Elizabeth her greatest triumph by beating back an invasion by Spain's dreaded Armada.

The queen's last years were troubled by conflict with Spain, Irish uprisings, and continued religious strife as Jesuit missionaries worked furtively to restore Catholicism and Puritans demanded a more radical Protestantism. Elizabeth also faced challenges from within her own court, notably from Robert Devereux, earl of Essex, who turned against her after falling from favor. But she weathered every storm. At her death in 1603 she left to her successor, James I, Mary Stuart's Protestant son, a greater and more secure nation, defying dire predictions that a virgin queen would fail to provide for England's future.

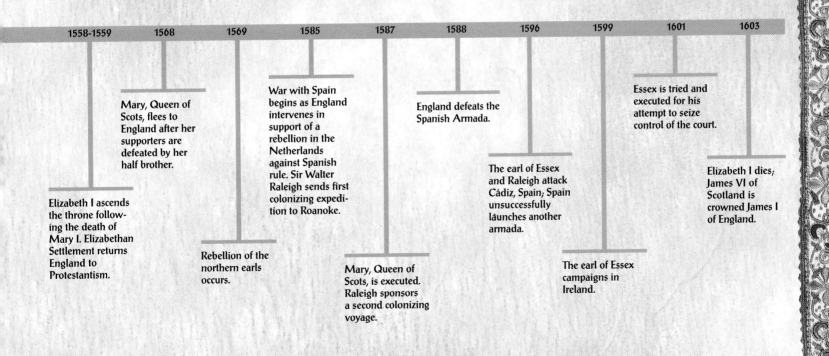

1558-1559 — Elizabeth I ascends the throne following the death of Mary I. Elizabethan Settlement returns England to Protestantism.

1568 — Mary, Queen of Scots, flees to England after her supporters are defeated by her half brother.

1569 — Rebellion of the northern earls occurs.

1585 — War with Spain begins as England intervenes in support of a rebellion in the Netherlands against Spanish rule. Sir Walter Raleigh sends first colonizing expedition to Roanoke.

1587 — Mary, Queen of Scots, is executed. Raleigh sponsors a second colonizing voyage.

1588 — England defeats the Spanish Armada.

1596 — The earl of Essex and Raleigh attack Cádiz, Spain; Spain unsuccessfully launches another armada.

1599 — The earl of Essex campaigns in Ireland.

1601 — Essex is tried and executed for his attempt to seize control of the court.

1603 — Elizabeth I dies; James VI of Scotland is crowned James I of England.

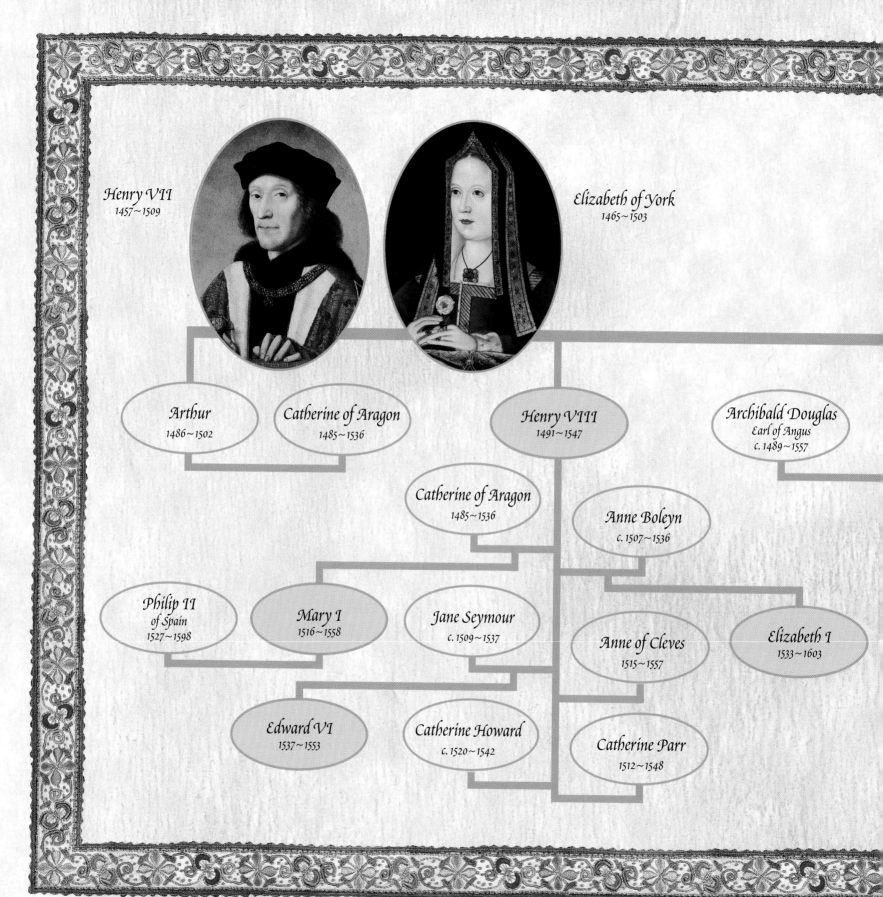

Henry VII
1457~1509

Elizabeth of York
1465~1503

Arthur
1486~1502

Catherine of Aragon
1485~1536

Henry VIII
1491~1547

Archibald Douglas
Earl of Angus
c. 1489~1557

Catherine of Aragon
1485~1536

Anne Boleyn
c. 1507~1536

Philip II
of Spain
1527~1598

Mary I
1516~1558

Jane Seymour
c. 1509~1537

Anne of Cleves
1515~1557

Elizabeth I
1533~1603

Edward VI
1537~1553

Catherine Howard
c. 1520~1542

Catherine Parr
1512~1548

The Tudor Royal Tree

In 1485, Henry Tudor, earl of Richmond, defeated and killed King Richard III at Bosworth Field. The earl then claimed the crown as Henry VII and married Elizabeth of York, daughter of Richard's deceased brother, Edward IV, thus fostering the Tudor dynasty.

This illustration of the Tudor family tree, with birth and death dates, shows the branchings that produced England's next six monarchs *(darkened ovals)*, including the doomed Jane Grey, who held the throne for just nine days in 1553. Marriages are indicated by connecting horizontal lines except in the case of the much-wedded Henry VIII. His six marriages are shown in chronological order on a vertical line.

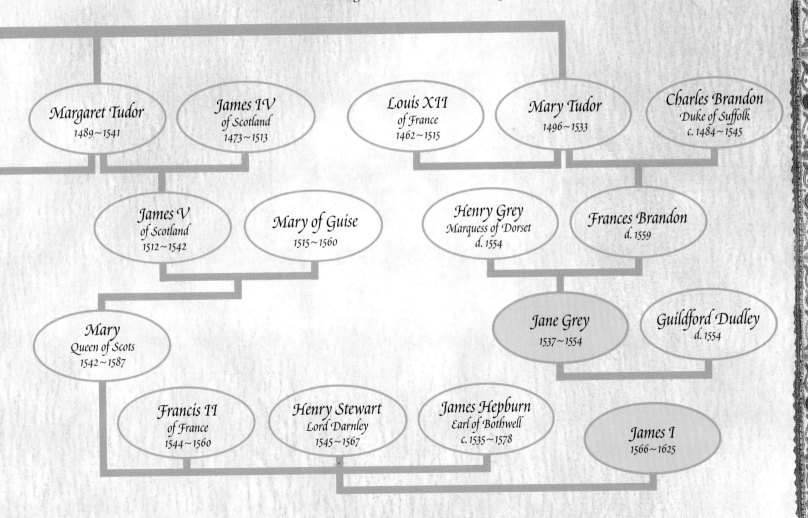

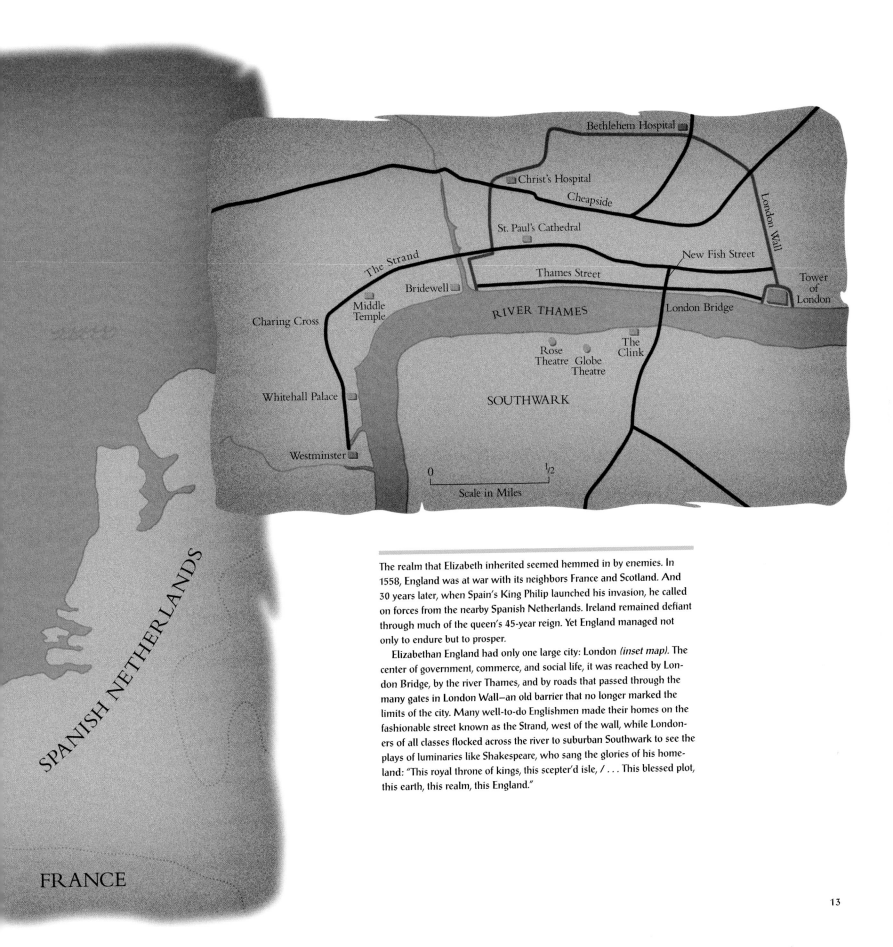

The realm that Elizabeth inherited seemed hemmed in by enemies. In 1558, England was at war with its neighbors France and Scotland. And 30 years later, when Spain's King Philip launched his invasion, he called on forces from the nearby Spanish Netherlands. Ireland remained defiant through much of the queen's 45-year reign. Yet England managed not only to endure but to prosper.

Elizabethan England had only one large city: London *(inset map)*. The center of government, commerce, and social life, it was reached by London Bridge, by the river Thames, and by roads that passed through the many gates in London Wall—an old barrier that no longer marked the limits of the city. Many well-to-do Englishmen made their homes on the fashionable street known as the Strand, west of the wall, while Londoners of all classes flocked across the river to suburban Southwark to see the plays of luminaries like Shakespeare, who sang the glories of his homeland: "This royal throne of kings, this scepter'd isle, / . . . This blessed plot, this earth, this realm, this England."

A Formidable Father

"Our king does not desire gold, or gems, or precious metal," remarked an English lord when Henry VIII came to power in 1509, "but virtue, glory, immortality." In years to come, Henry's pursuit of glory would convulse England and leave great issues to be confronted by his daughter and eventual successor, Elizabeth.

Young Henry had brilliant prospects. Just 18 at the time of his coronation, he inherited a stable realm from his father,

Bearded and bejeweled, Henry VIII stands confidently in this flattering portrait of the grossly overweight king painted by Hans Holbein in 1540.

Henry VII, founder of the Tudor dynasty, and he enhanced his position by marrying his brother's widow, Catherine of Aragon, daughter of King Ferdinand and Queen Isabella of Spain, the most powerful nation in Europe. A true Renaissance man, he read Greek and Latin and composed music and verse, but he delighted above all in sport, pageantry, and feasting. As he wrote in one of his poems: "Pastime with good company / I love and shall until I die."

The first English king to insist on being addressed as "Your Majesty," Henry claimed unprecedented powers during his reign. He set himself up as supreme head of the Church of England after the pope refused to annul his marriage to Catherine. He then closed the monasteries and used their assets to reward his favorites and help fund his foreign campaigns.

Henry left a mixed legacy, strengthening the monarchy but provoking unrest at home and hostility abroad. Ultimately, it fell to Elizabeth to reckon with the consequences of his tumultuous career.

Scepter in hand, Henry proceeds to Parliament in 1512 accompanied by lords carrying symbols of their office. Henry used Parliament as he saw fit, calling it into session to raise taxes for his wars and to confirm his position as head of the church.

Henry's Quest for an Heir

Henry VIII shatters his lance triumphantly against his opponent's helmet in a tournament in 1511 celebrating the birth of his son, the short-lived Prince Henry, to Catherine of Aragon, shown here reclining on a bed. Of several children born to the royal couple, only Mary survived infancy.

Although Henry VIII had six wives, he might have been content with the first, Catherine of Aragon, if she had given him a healthy male heir. Their only surviving child, Mary, would undoubtedly wed a foreign king or prince who would bend her to his own will. Henry wanted a successor in his own image, one who would be master of the realm and perpetuate the Tudor name.

Matters erupted in January 1533 when Henry learned that his mistress, Anne Boleyn, was pregnant, and he promptly married her—without getting an annulment from Rome of his union with Catherine. In May the archbishop of Canterbury, Thomas Cranmer, declared Henry's marriage to Catherine invalid because it defied a biblical decree against a man taking his brother's

wife. This left Henry forever at odds with Rome and made Mary illegitimate.

On September 7, 1533, despite assurances from court doctors and astrologers that a boy was due, Anne gave birth to a daughter, Elizabeth. "By God's grace, boys will follow," Henry told Anne. But when no children were forthcoming, he abandoned her to her enemies at court, who convicted her on dubious charges that included several counts of adultery and incest with her brother. Anne was beheaded in 1536, and Elizabeth, like Mary, lost her place in the line of succession. Within days of the execution, Henry wed Jane Seymour, who bore him his long-awaited prince, Edward, but died shortly after giving birth.

Edward was Henry's last child, but he had three more wives: Anne of Cleves, whom he found so unappealing that he failed to consummate the union; the wayward 17-year-old Catherine Howard, beheaded for adultery in 1542; and the virtuous Catherine Parr, who dealt kindly with Mary and Elizabeth. Before his death, Henry restored his two daughters to the line of succession after Edward.

Seeking Glory Abroad

Henry's foreign affairs were as turbulent as his domestic ones. He began his reign firmly allied with Spain, aided by his marriage to the Spanish princess Catherine. But his rejection of Catherine—and Catholicism—strained relations between England and Spain and set the stage for later conflict.

Toward France, Henry was hostile from the start. "Magnificent, liberal, and a great enemy of the French," wrote the Venetian ambassador of Henry on his coronation day. He hoped to win glory by regaining former English territories across the Channel and waged two wars against France for that purpose. In between, he met with the French king, Francis I, holding grand parleys like the one at right, which failed to reconcile the two. "These sovereigns," noted one observer, "hate each other very cordially."

Scotland—allied with France and intent on remaining independent from England—was another thorn in Henry's side. His costly war against Scotland in the 1540s resembled his other campaigns in that the gains he achieved were fleeting and the animosities he stirred up were lasting. He left his successors with depleted resources at home and determined enemies abroad.

Henry VIII, astride a white horse, and 6,000 Englishmen parade past a palace he built in France in 1520 for a week-long meeting with King Francis I at the Field of Cloth of Gold, named for the material decorating France's tents.

The Line of Succession

"The King is dead," cried heralds on January 31, 1547, when Henry VIII breathed his last. "Long live the King!" But Henry's son and successor, nine-year-old Edward VI, would not live long. By the spring of 1553, he was near death from consumption and due to be succeeded by his 37-year-old sister Mary, a fervent Catholic. To prevent that, advisers persuaded Edward to set aside both Mary and Elizabeth as illegitimate and designate as his heir Henry's great-niece, Lady Jane Grey, who shared Edward's religious convictions.

Jane reluctantly ascended the throne after Edward's death on July 6 and ruled for only nine days before being deposed by Mary, who enjoyed support both from Catholics and from Protestants loyal to Henry. Jane was later beheaded after refusing to seek clemency by embracing Catholicism; many others fell victim to "Bloody Mary," as the queen was remembered. Her decision to wed Philip, heir to the Spanish throne, prompted an uprising by those who feared Spanish domination and wanted to replace Mary with Elizabeth (already in an awkward position as the daughter of the notorious Anne Boleyn, who had blighted Mary's youth). The 20-year-old Elizabeth was held in the Tower of London on suspicion of involvement in the plot but protested her innocence and, unlike the rebels, escaped with her head.

Mary's ensuing campaign to restore Catholicism and persecute heretics came as a shock even to some who shared her beliefs. By her authority, more than 270 people, including Archbishop Cranmer, were burned at the stake for heresy. Although Elizabeth went along with Mary by attending Catholic Mass, she was recognized by Protestants as one of their own. As a popular poet later wrote of Mary's victims: "When these with violence were burned to death, / We wished for our Elizabeth."

Those wishes were granted in November 1558 when Mary died childless after reluctantly confirming Elizabeth as her heir in order to please Philip, who hoped to wed Elizabeth himself or match her with another prominent Spaniard. But Philip and others who tried to control the new queen were in for a surprise. Even as she wrestled with the problems bequeathed to her, Elizabeth fulfilled the high hopes that King Henry had had for his son by ruling her realm with a firm hand—and yielding to no man.

Future Tudor queens Mary *(far left)* and Elizabeth *(near right)* wait in the wings as Henry VIII embraces his cherished son and heir, Edward, in the symbolic presence of Edward's mother, Jane Seymour, who in fact died soon after delivering the boy.

CHAPTER ONE

The Queen
and Her Court

Queen Elizabeth rides in her litter in a wedding procession through London in 1600, supported effortlessly by her courtiers, including the bridegroom in white, gesturing toward his bride. Although Elizabeth was in her sixties at the time of this ceremony, she was portrayed as a youthful and ethereal virgin queen.

he queen was angry. All through the month of October 1566, Elizabeth's anger rose, seeping icily into the gilded galleries of Whitehall Palace along the Thames River west of London and filling her great privy chamber, where the painted image of her father, Henry VIII, looked down on her worried councilors and courtiers with hard little eyes, as if to remind them that the Tudors were not to be trifled with.

Members of Parliament would never have dared to pry into her father's royal concerns, but they were prying into hers. They planned to present the queen with a petition, asking the 33-year-old Elizabeth to marry and name a successor, in case she died without producing an heir. Her personal feelings aside, Elizabeth regarded this as a confidential matter of state, not fit for public debate. To make matters worse, the House of Commons proposed to link the petition to a bill providing subsidies for the Crown. The queen's natural allies in the House of Lords, including noblemen and bishops of the Church of England, could not prevent that maneuver, nor did they wish to, for they too were concerned about the succession.

Elizabeth had the power to suspend Parliament and send the members home to cool down for a few months. But as one councilor pointed out to her, that would simply allow them to tell their constituents that the queen took them for granted and wanted Parliament to do "nothing but give away your money." If there was one thing Elizabeth prized above all, it was the good opinion of her subjects.

The queen's anger reached its peak in late October when leaders of the House of Lords gathered in her presence to urge her to name her successor. How dare these nobles, so protective of their own privileges, interfere in a matter that was hers to decide? Elizabeth called the duke of Norfolk a traitor (a charge that would come back to haunt him) and told the marquess of Northampton, who had faced questions about the validity of his second marriage, to mind his own affairs.

She had sharp words as well for Robert Dudley, her favorite at court, whom she had recently raised to the nobility by making him earl of Leicester. Long the queen's Master of the Horse—and still the master of her heart, many said—he knew Elizabeth would never consent to marry him, but he retained her affection, and she asked from him in return absolute loyalty. All the world might abandon her, she said, but she expected better of him. He vowed that he would die at her feet, but his gallantry left her cold. She needed staunch defenders, not swooning courtiers. Elizabeth walked out on the lords and briefly considered placing them under house arrest.

If no one would help her, she would have to bring Parliament to heel on her own. In early November, she summoned 30 members from each house to an audience. The proud men who obeyed her summons regarded the queen with some ambivalence. As their monarch she commanded their respect, but as a woman she seemed to them sorely in need of guidance. They considered it unnatural and irresponsible of her to refuse marriage. Women needed husbands. The country needed an heir to the throne, if not one born to the queen then one designated by her. What if Elizabeth died, as she nearly had from smallpox four years earlier? England might descend into savage warfare between Catholics and Protestants of the sort that would engulf France and the Low Countries for decades to come.

Members of Parliament, most of them Protestants like Elizabeth, had good reason to fear such strife in the event of her death. She was the last living child of Henry VIII, and unless she produced an heir or named one, no one would have a stronger claim to the throne than her cousin Mary Stuart, queen of Scots, the granddaughter of Henry's older sister, Margaret Tudor, and King James IV of Scotland. Mary was everything English

Elizabeth presides over the opening of Parliament from her throne in the House of Lords, made up of richly dressed nobles and bishops. Standing at the bar at bottom are members of the House of Commons, composed of gentlemen of less than noble rank who were elected by their fellow landholders. Parliament convened only when called by the queen, who could not raise taxes or enact laws without its approval.

Protestants dreaded: a firm Catholic, with close ties to hostile France and an appeal to Catholics in northern England, a stronghold of the Roman faith. Protestants wanted an heir of their own persuasion put forward to keep Mary, who had recently wed her English-born cousin and produced a son, from succeeding Elizabeth, a calamity the very "stones in the street would rebel against," as one of them put it.

But Elizabeth saw the matter differently. She did not feel a pressing need to name a successor because she had no intention of dying any time soon. Among the ranks of richly dressed dignitaries who faced her in the fading light of that November afternoon were men far older than the queen. She appeared before them in her prime, graced with a trim figure, long slender hands, dazzling reddish gold hair, and a fashionably pale complexion scarcely blemished by her bout with the dreaded smallpox.

They had blundered, she told them. Hotheads in the Commons had put the delicate matter of the succession into public debate, and though it was the duty of the Lords to curb such impertinence, they had followed the pack. They gave the impression that the queen was ignoring England's welfare. "Was I not born in the realm?" she demanded. "Is there any cause I should alienate myself from being careful over this country? Is not my kingdom here?" She had indicated that she would take a husband if it pleased God and served the interests of her realm, and her statements had been disregarded. "A strange order of petitioners," she declared, who would ask for her word, "and yet will not believe it when it is spoken!"

She added that those who were hurrying her into marriage would be just as quick to disparage her husband if she took one. No one in the chamber could deny this. Although various foreign kings and princes had been proposed as candidates for her hand, many in England feared that a consort from abroad would entangle the realm in dangerous alliances and conflicts and were sure to denounce such a match, as they had when Elizabeth's sister and predecessor, Mary Tudor, wed Philip of Spain. And there might be just as great an outcry if Elizabeth settled on an English husband, as evidenced by strong opposition to Dudley's suit.

If she could not find a husband to their liking, why should her choice of a successor be any less controversial? And what would prevent the queen's enemies from rallying around that successor and plotting against her? Elizabeth knew the danger of that all too well, for in her youth she had been next in line to her sister, and some in Parliament—whom she would not name for her honor's sake—had tried to involve her in treasonous plots to depose Mary. If she settled on a successor, the result might be civil war, imperiling all those in authority. It was not that she herself feared death. "Though I be a woman," she insisted, "yet I have as good a courage, answerable to my place, as ever my father had." But she would not subvert the God-given order of her realm by yielding to the rash demands of those beneath her.

"I am your anointed Queen," she reminded her listeners pointedly. "I will never be by violence constrained to do anything. I thank God I am indeed endowed with such qualities that if I were turned out of the realm in my petticoat, I were able to live in any place in Christendom." One day she might name a successor, Elizabeth allowed, but only when the time was right and not in response to a petition from below, "for it is monstrous that the feet should direct the head."

She then dismissed her subjects. Stunned by her fervor—and perhaps a bit dazed by the vision of their anointed queen wandering abroad in her petticoat—the 60 members of Parliament left without saying a word. She had never given them a chance.

Elizabeth's Religious Settlement

Having been confined to the Tower by her sister, Mary, before becoming queen, Elizabeth thanked God for leading her "from the prison to the palace." Her Protestant subjects were equally grateful when she succeeded Mary in 1558. They looked to Elizabeth to resume the English Reformation of her father, Henry VIII, and her brother, Edward VI. But she knew that many in her realm remained Catholics at heart, and she had no wish to alienate them by reforming the Church of England too much. As head of the church, she hoped to reconcile her divided nation by seeking a middle ground between Catholicism and the strict Protestantism of those who would become known as Puritans.

She made this so-called Elizabethan Settlement her highest priority. Just three months into her reign, she called Parliament into session to enact "laws for the according and uniting of the people into a uniform order of religion." The resulting legislation reflected the queen's hopeful vision of a new Protestant church that would appeal to those of the old faith.

For Elizabeth, this was a matter of personal conviction as much as political convenience. She shared such Protestant principles as the belief that worshipers should receive the word of God in English rather than in Latin, a language few in her realm fully understood. At the same time, she admired many of the customs and ceremonies of Catholicism and hoped to preserve them in her reformed church.

She kept up hallowed traditions observed since medieval times, such as washing the feet of the poor on Maundy Thursday and soothing with her royal touch those suffering from scrofula, the "king's evil." And she favored the display of crucifixes and candles in places of worship, rejecting Protestant views that such objects were idolatrous. Once, when the dean of St. Paul's Cathedral began preaching to that effect, she interrupted him in mid-sermon and told him to drop the subject. As part of the religious settlement, candles and crucifixes were retained in churches, but religious statuary and paintings were removed or whitewashed. Elizabeth also favored traditional sacred music in church and employed Catholic composers in her Chapel Royal.

Although she may have agreed with Catholics that priests should remain celibate, she yielded to Protestant demands that

Embracing the Protestant view that the Scriptures should be widely accessible, Elizabeth authorized a new version in English, with a frontispiece showing her image.

Emulating earlier Catholic monarchs, Elizabeth kneels at prayer in her private chapel *(left)* and, in imitation of Christ, prepares to wash the feet of the poor on Maundy Thursday, while an attendant holds her long purple train *(inset)*.

Protestants gather at the table that replaced the high altar in the Church of England so that all could partake of the bread and wine that represented the flesh and blood of Christ. In the Catholic Mass, only priests drank the wine.

English clergymen be allowed to marry, while insisting that their prospective wives be inspected and approved. Other notable departures from Catholic practice included changes in the liturgy to involve the congregation more fully in services and an increased emphasis on sermons, although Elizabeth herself hated preachers who went on too long.

One Puritanical notion that she would not abide was that ministers should dispense with clerical dress. The Elizabethan Settlement specified that all clergy in the Church of England should wear robes, and Elizabeth once chided a bishop who opposed that rule by remarking to him pointedly, "That loose gown becomes you mighty well."

Tenor
Morning prayer.
This tenor is for men.

Ome let vs sing vnto the Lord let vs
reioyce in the strength of our saluation let
come before his presence with thankes geuing and shew our
in him with psalmes. For the Lord
aboue all

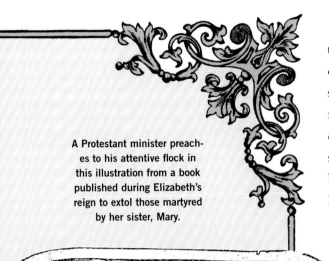

A Protestant minister preaches to his attentive flock in this illustration from a book published during Elizabeth's reign to extol those martyred by her sister, Mary.

This prayer with English lyrics sung in Elizabethan times represents a Protestant version of the old Catholic tradition of matins, or morning devotions.

Elizabeth's stirring performance brought the House of Lords into line. Members of the Commons took exception, however, when she ordered them not to discuss the issue of succession. In time, she heeded counsel and offered concessions, revoking her order of silence and reducing by one-third the requested subsidy for the Crown. The Commons received this with hearty prayers and thanks and left off discussing the succession. But they did attach a preamble to the tax bill, recording Elizabeth's willingness to name a successor. Ever vigilant when it came to legislation, she withheld her assent and noted on the bill, "I know no reason why any of my private answers to the realm should serve for prologue to a subsidies book." The Commons duly amended the preamble to her satisfaction.

By sheer eloquence and determination, she had fended off a commitment she regarded as disagreeable and dangerous. But the concerns that led Parliament to press her on the matter would not go away. Ultimately, Elizabeth would have to reckon with the challenge posed by her Catholic cousin and the rebellious schemes Mary inspired.

Members of Parliament were not the only ones to feel the queen's fury. Those at court who attended her over the years grew all too familiar with her fits of temper, which alternated with dazzling displays of charm. "When she smiles, it was a pure sunshine that everyone did choose to bask in if they could," wrote one of her courtiers, "but anon came a storm from a sudden gathering of clouds, and the thunder fell in wondrous manner on all alike."

Perhaps her volatile nature stemmed in part from the strains of her early years. She scarcely knew her mother, Anne Boleyn, who was beheaded for adultery in 1536—when Elizabeth was not yet three—after being forsaken by the once-adoring Henry and plotted against by his courtiers. In the aftermath of her mother's execution, little Elizabeth sensed the change in her status. "How haps it, Governor," she asked one of her guardians after Henry had her declared illegitimate and removed from the line of succession, "yesterday my Lady Princess, and today but my Lady Elizabeth?" Although her father sent her to live away from court, he supported her in style and dispatched a courtier to wish her a happy Christmas when she was six. Elizabeth gave "humble thanks" for the king's blessing, the courtier reported back, "enquiring again of his Majesty's welfare, and that with as great a gravity as she had been forty years old."

Although preoccupied with his male heir, Edward, Henry eventually restored Elizabeth to the line of succession, and she received one of the finest educations his kingdom could afford. A voracious reader, she was brilliantly tutored by a team of Protestant, hu-

INFLUENCE OF THE STARS

Elizabeth's royal astrologer, John Dee *(right)*, played an important role at court at a time when rich and poor alike believed that the constellations and other heavenly bodies influenced the course of events and held clues to the future. Dee was advising Elizabeth long before she asked him to select an auspicious date for her coronation—January 15, 1559. Several years earlier, while confined in the Tower of London by order of her sister, Queen Mary, she had him cast her horoscope and was comforted by his prediction that she would one day return to court in power. Later, Dee counseled her as queen on matters ranging from the portent of a comet to the prognosis for a royal toothache (bodily ailments were thought to be governed by the signs of the zodiac).

But Dee was more than just a stargazer and soothsayer. He defined astrology as "an art mathematical" and made keen observations and calculations that advanced navigation and other scientific pursuits in this age of discovery.

manist scholars from Cambridge University. She mastered Greek and Latin (later delivering extemporaneous speeches in Latin as queen) and became fluent as well in French and Italian. She learned to charm in ladylike fashion by singing and dancing gracefully and playing instruments, but she also shared her father's love of sports and excelled as a rider and hunter.

Henry's death early in 1547, when Elizabeth was 13, placed her younger brother, Edward, on the throne and left her in the care of her father's last wife, Catherine Parr, who had helped reconcile Henry to his daughters. Catherine soon found a new husband, the reckless and devilishly handsome Thomas Seymour, Lord High Admiral of England, who seemed less interested in

his wife than in her royal stepdaughter. At times, he would slip into Elizabeth's bedchamber in his nightgown and romp with her, leading her governess to complain that it was indecent for such a man to come "bare-legged to a maid's chamber."

Elizabeth was sent off to another house, but the trouble did not end there. Following Catherine's death from complications related to childbirth in 1548, Seymour renewed his pursuit of Elizabeth and may even have proposed marriage. His passion for her was more than personal. He hoped to gain power not only by marrying an heir to the throne but also by scheming against his own brother, who served as Lord Protector to the young king Edward. That plot unraveled, and Seymour was condemned and beheaded for treason in 1549. Before his execution, Elizabeth underwent lengthy questioning. She stoutly denied any knowledge of his treasonous schemes and denounced as "shameful slanders" rumors that she was pregnant by Seymour. The danger to which he exposed her, combined with the memory of her mother's fate, left her all the more cautious when it came to future courtships. But she evidently liked Seymour's type. Throughout her life, she would exhibit a fondness for men at court who possessed similar qualities—adventurous, suave, and often scheming.

The next few years were relatively tranquil for Elizabeth, who seemed to share King Edward's Protestant convictions and acted the part by behaving and

involvement in a revolt that broke out in early 1554 when Mary decided to wed Philip of Spain, who was opposed by Protestants both as a foreigner and as a Catholic (at one point, Londoners heaved snowballs at his envoys in the streets). In March, after the revolt had fizzled, the 20-year-old Elizabeth was conducted by barge to the Tower of London, where enemies of the Crown were held. "Here landeth as true a subject, being prisoner, as ever landed at these stairs," she reportedly declared as she stepped ashore, "and before thee, O God, I speak it, having no friends but thee alone." Several of the warders assigned to watch over the young woman knelt at her feet, and one of them cried out, "God preserve your Grace!"

"*Here landeth as true a subject, being prisoner, as ever landed at these stairs.*"

dressing modestly (a sign of piety among those who rejected Catholicism and its colorful vestments and ceremonies). Her plain dress may also have been meant to counter the rumors of her involvement with Seymour and signal that she was chaste. Edward called her his "sweet sister temperance," and once sent 200 horsemen to conduct her to court. It showed, one Catholic ambassador sourly remarked, "how much glory belongs to her who has embraced the new religion and is become a very great lady."

That was not the best position to be in when Edward died in 1553 and Elizabeth's devoutly Catholic sister, Mary, claimed the throne after ousting their Protestant cousin, Lady Jane Grey, whom Edward had named as his heir in defiance of Henry's will. Elizabeth's plain dresses were now out of fashion, and Mary sent her fine clothes and jewelry to wear.

Elizabeth tried to please Mary by requesting instruction in Catholicism. But that did not shield her from suspicion of

So kind were the warders to Elizabeth that the Constable of the Tower, a strict Catholic, eventually cut back her privileges, which included deliveries of extra provisions to her chamber and frequent walks with her attendants along the battlements. All the while, she was in grave peril. The leader of the failed plot, Thomas Wyatt, was tortured in a futile effort to extract from him a confession incriminating Elizabeth; he was executed in April. More than one envoy at court advised Mary to have her sister beheaded.

Elizabeth feared that she might meet the same fate her mother had suffered at the Tower 18 years earlier. In May, when a party of men in armor arrived there from court, she had reason to suspect that her execution was imminent—only to learn that she was being transferred to house arrest at a manor in Oxfordshire, where she would remain for a year before regaining her freedom. Along the way, church bells pealed, and cheering crowds showered her with cakes and other confections.

All this came as an education for Elizabeth in the art of survival. She learned how perilous it could be for a reigning queen to have a popular successor waiting in the wings, inspiring plots willingly or not. She learned to trim the truth when necessary—and to stand up to her accusers when pressed and never to waver in her own defense. She learned to cherish the support of the common people, who were true to her in adversity. And she learned to distrust the fickle affections of those at court. In November 1558, as Mary lay dying at St. James's Palace in London, courtiers left the queen in droves and flocked to pay their respects to her successor Elizabeth at Hatfield House, many miles away, clogging the route with their horses and wagons. Elizabeth never forgot their unseemly haste. Mary, she would say, had been "buried alive" by her faithless followers long before her heart stopped.

Nearly two months would elapse between Elizabeth's accession to power and her coronation, a lavish ceremony that required elaborate preparations. In the meantime, she had serious matters of state to consider. The kingdom she inherited from her sister was in disarray. Mary's punishing campaign to reunite England spiritually under the authority of the pope had only deepened the divide between Catholics and Protestants. And her unpopular husband, Philip, had lured her into an ill-considered war against France that cost the English control of Calais, their last possession across the Channel, and further depleted a royal treasury already reduced by Henry's campaigns. As a veteran official glumly summarized the situation facing Mary's successor: "The Queen poor, the realm exhausted . . . The people out of order."

William Cecil, Elizabeth's most trusted adviser and her principal secretary for the first part of her reign, holds his staff of office as Lord Treasurer, the post he assumed after she raised him to the nobility as Baron Burghley. She also made him a knight of the Garter, an honorary order whose regalia included lush red robes.

Elizabeth's first step in restoring order was to appoint trusted men to her Privy Council to advise her and administer England's affairs. To serve as her principal secretary and chief councilor, she chose William Cecil, who at 38 had already distinguished himself in law, politics, and diplomacy. Although renowned for his discretion, Cecil had not always been so prudent. As a young gentleman of good family—not of noble rank but important enough to aspire to a place at court—he had angered his father by marrying a girl of modest means whose mother tended a wineshop, and his education at Cambridge was cut short. As if to atone for that rash deed, he went on to conform to the highest expectations by studying law in London, winning election to the House of Commons, and taking as a second wife after the death of his first the accomplished daughter of a rising courtier to King Edward, whom Cecil subsequently served at court. A Protestant, he survived Queen Mary's reign by wearing a rosary and carrying out brief diplomatic missions.

Such pragmatism endeared him to Elizabeth, who hoped to avoid religious warfare by charting a middle course for the Church of England between Catholicism and the extreme form of Protestantism that became known during her reign as Puritanism. Similarly, she wanted to avoid foreign conflicts, at least until England was stronger. Cecil served Elizabeth well in both areas, but he did not always agree with her. When she appointed him, she expressed confidence that "without respect of my private will, you will give me that counsel which you think best." In years to come, he did just that, sometimes angering her in the process. She, in turn, often exasperated Cecil by procrastinating on such issues as marriage and the succession. But she repaid him for his pains by naming him to profitable posts and eventually raising him to the nobility as Baron Burghley.

Aside from such rewards, members of the Privy Council could expect little in the way of thanks. If a policy succeeded, the Crown must get the credit; if it failed, the council must take the blame. Elizabeth had seen her sister Mary stripped of her royal aura of infallibility, and she was determined to avoid the same fate. While she worked with her councilors to put England's affairs back in order, she would do all she could to endear herself to her people and retain their love.

The remarkable rapport between Elizabeth and her subjects was evident as soon as her accession was announced. The bells of London pealed in wild cacophony, and at night, a thousand bonfires lit the sky. Elizabeth fanned the fervor by riding through the city or gliding along the Thames in her gilded barge. "If ever any person had either the gift or the style to win the hearts of the people," reported one chronicler, "it was this Queen."

Not all in England were so jubilant. In the predominantly Catholic north, many people feared her Protestant leanings, but she had neither the time nor the inclination to visit that disaffected region. Her first concern was to rally her loving subjects in and around London. The celebrations reached their peak with her coronation on January 15, 1559, a date selected as auspicious by the royal astrologer, John Dee. The horoscope for the date may have been favorable, but the skies above London on the eve of the great event were foreboding. Snow fell on the Saturday of her coronation procession to Westminster Abbey, where she would be crowned on Sunday. Nonetheless, the city bustled and bloomed, as if roused by Elizabeth's radiance. Tapestries and velvets hung from wooden railings along the streets, and bright banners dangled from the upper windows of the houses.

At intervals along the route stood wooden stages for pageants—allegorical scenes representing the virtues of the new queen and her Protestant faith. Among the themes portrayed were Unity and Concord (with figures of Elizabeth's Tudor forebears, including Anne Boleyn); Time and his daughter Truth (who presented Elizabeth with an English Bible); and the biblical Deborah ("judge and restorer of the House of Israel" and a noted example of a woman exercising authority). Each pageant featured musicians and a charming young narrator, there to recite explanatory verses to the crowd and to Elizabeth herself when she paused along the way.

She was dazzling to behold, costumed in cloth of gold trimmed with ermine and seated on a litter draped with gold brocade and lined with white satin. On either side walked her honor guard of gentlemen pensioners, carrying gilded battle-axes. Riding closely in her wake was her handsome Master of the Horse, Robert Dudley. Before and behind her litter paraded hundreds of brightly clad courtiers.

Time and again Elizabeth stopped the litter in the press of people, to speak to one well-wisher or another or to cry, "God thank you all." She hushed the crowds at pageants so that she could hear the youngsters recite. She was endlessly patient with her beloved commoners, indulging those who went on too long or spoke out of turn. "Remember old King Harry the Eighth!" shouted one man during the procession, drawing from Elizabeth a smile that warmed the crowd. No gesture was too small to warrant her attention. She carried a sprig of rosemary given her by a poor woman all the way to Westminster.

On Sunday, Elizabeth walked in procession from Whitehall across a blue carpet to Westminster Abbey, emerging later a crowned queen with orb and scepter to greet her boisterous admirers—who had cut the carpet into thousands of pieces for keepsakes. One foreign observer thought her too indulgent with the crowd. "In my opinion," he wrote crossly, "she exceeded the bounds of gravity and decorum." But to those who thronged the streets to hail their new queen, her gracious familiarity only increased her dignity and heightened their esteem.

The brilliance of Elizabeth's coronation, enhanced by her warmth and charm, set the tone for her reign. She saw it as her duty to be glorious, to shine like the sun on her followers and nourish their devotion. Nowhere was her radiance more evident than in the splendor of her court.

The queen and her retinue had many palaces to choose from. Her royal inheritance included dozens of castles, many of which she left to decay, and innumerable manor houses, most of which she leased out. She and her royal entourage kept largely to the finest of her properties, a string of palatial residences along the Thames, moving from one to another in a seasonal round

A coach bearing Elizabeth nears Nonsuch, so called because it was like no other palace in England. Built by her father, Henry VIII, the small but grand retreat southwest of London was the queen's favorite place for riding and hunting. Her courtiers were less fond of it, however, because some of them had to sleep in tents set up in the courtyard.

determined partly by ceremony and partly by more practical concerns. The queen's hundreds of followers quickly depleted local food supplies and fouled the area with their waste, raising the specter of epidemics. When Elizabeth and company moved on to the next stop, the vacated palace and grounds could be tidied up and the stocks replenished.

In the summer, the queen usually went on progress, touring the countryside with her councilors and courtiers and staying at the homes of dignitaries. In the fall, she held court at Whitehall, whose assorted gatehouses, galleries, and gardens covered 23 acres

along the Thames. There she often spent Christmas and New Year's Day—an occasion for gift giving—but went elsewhere for other festivities and diversions, including the hunts she relished.

Easternmost of her river palaces was Greenwich, Elizabeth's birthplace, from whose windows she could watch ships heading out to sea and wave them on. Upriver from Greenwich lay London and Whitehall, and beyond that, amid tranquil meadows and wending waters crowded with swans and herons, rose the towers and onion domes of Richmond Palace, nestled

amid orchards. Built by Elizabeth's grandfather, Henry VII, that grand retreat had no fewer than 18 kitchens. It was less drafty than other palaces—"a warm nest for my old age," Elizabeth called it—and had fresh water piped in from springs. Farther up-river stood Hampton Court, grandly embellished by Henry VIII, and Windsor Castle. And the countryside around was dotted with other royal palaces such as Oatlands and Henry VIII's fantasy, Nonsuch, much favored for hunting.

Among the diversions at one palace or another were gardens and courtyards, enclosed galleries hundreds of feet long for strolls on rainy days, tennis courts, tiltyards for jousting, and cockpits and bear pits. The queen herself avoided cockfights, deemed unsuitable for ladies, but took a keen interest in bearbaiting and owned mastiffs that competed against bears in the pit. (Common people enjoyed such blood sports as well, and Elizabeth gratified them by vetoing a bill supported by Puritans in Parliament that would have banned bearbaiting and other diversions on Sunday.)

Each palace when occupied was a great hive of activity, at the heart of which lay the queen's own compartments. The largest of these was her presence chamber, designed for public ceremonies. The one at Hampton Court, dubbed the Paradise Chamber, boasted a throne of brown velvet worked with gold and set with diamonds and a precious collection of musical instruments that included one virginal, or small harpsichord, made of glass and another with gold and silver strings. Meetings of a more confidential nature convened in the queen's privy chamber, and the most sensitive matters were often discussed in her bedchamber, reached only by trusted confidants admitted by her guards.

She seldom received such visitors early in the day. By her own admission, she was "not a morning woman." She worked late and often rose late, and sometimes lingered for a while at her window, listening to the gossip in the gardens below and occasionally joining in. Unlike most people in her realm, she had ample opportunity to bathe—amid mirrored walls and ceilings at Windsor. She favored a perfume of rose water and cleansed her teeth with toothpicks and cloths, perhaps rinsing her mouth afterward with one of the popular breath sweeteners of the day, such as rosemary and cinnamon. Late in her reign, her godson, John Harington, devised an innovative water closet that may have been installed at one of her palaces. Otherwise, she made do with a chamber pot, housed in a portable close-stool with a velvet-covered seat. The task of emptying the chamber pot was traditionally entrusted to a royal attendant called the Groom of the Stool. In Elizabeth's case, one of her ladies handled that delicate responsibility.

Dressing the queen could take her attendants two hours. Simply selecting the right gown could be a chore, for Elizabeth had acquired hundreds. She sometimes dressed with plain elegance, but on ceremonial occasions, her preparations were elaborate. Underneath she often donned a corset and a hoop skirt called a farthingale. Her dresses came in sundry shades, and she wore them with great ropes of pearls and other jewelry. Soon after her coronation, she was introduced to the latest in fashion—formfitting silk stockings. She pronounced them "fine and delicate" and greatly preferred them to cloth hose.

"I do not live in a corner, a thousand eyes see all I do."

A Priuie in perfection.
Here is the same all put together, that the worke-
man may see if it be well.

PLUMBING FOR THE PALACE

In 1596 John Harington, Elizabeth's godson and a noted figure at court, devised "a privie in perfection" for royal use. As diagramed above, this water closet featured an elevated cistern, a wooden seat, and a valve that flushed water from the cistern down through the basin and out through a drainpipe so that "your worst privie may be as sweet as your best chamber," as Harington put it.

His invention was reportedly installed at one of the queen's palaces, but with no system for treating the sewage from the drainpipe, Harington's water closet did little to remedy the sanitation problem that forced the court to move often through the year.

The queen was seldom idle. According to one courtier, her daily exercise consisted of "six or seven galliards of a morning, besides music and singing." The simplest form of the galliard consisted of five brisk steps followed by a leap in the air during which dancers beat their feet together. (Elizabeth reportedly danced the men's steps of the galliard in private because they were more vigorous than the women's steps.) Much of her day, the same courtier added, was devoted to matters of state such as "reading letters, ordering answers, considering what should be brought before the council, and consulting with her ministers." Later on, "she would walk in a shady garden or pleasant gallery, without any other attendants than a few learned men; then she took coach and passed, in the sight of her people, to the neighbouring groves and fields, and sometimes would hunt and hawk." In the evenings, there might be entertainments at the palace, including dances, plays, and on festive occasions, fireworks.

Unlike her father, Elizabeth remained trim by eating lightly, often dining privately in her bedchamber. She liked fowl and fine white bread. She hated the dark heavy ale so popular in her realm, described by one chronicler as "old beer that will make a cat speak and a wise man dumb." Instead, she favored a younger, lighter beer, and had fresh supplies of it delivered to her when she was on progress.

"I do not live in a corner," Elizabeth once remarked, "a thousand eyes see all I do." To be sure, many of those who observed her at court did so from a respectful distance. Their ranks included large numbers of servants who attended not to the queen herself but to her courtiers, some of whom were peers of the realm and sat in the House of Lords. In all of England, there were only about 60 peers. They had their own lavish residences, often including palaces in London, but many lived at court for at least part of the year and sought official appointments there or other favors that might profit them. (Like the queen herself, they had steep expenses and welcomed additional income.) Similarly, distinguished gentlemen of less than noble rank came to court in search of offices or favors, including tax exemptions, land grants, manufacturing or mining monopolies, or rights to collect customs on imports. Favor seekers wore fancy clothes to attract the queen's notice, sent her gifts, and offered her petitions with worshipful solemnity when she marched in procession to chapel on Sundays.

Few at court knew the queen better than the married ladies and maids of honor who helped to dress her and otherwise saw to her comfort. Elizabeth liked to have pretty faces around, and her fetching young maids drew attention from the many gallant and footloose men at court. But the queen kept a sharp eye on her girls, querying them as to their suitors and striking them if they threatened to get out of line. They faced dismissal or worse if they became pregnant or married without her permission; in some cases, she had the men who wed them imprisoned. Such severity may have stemmed in part from her fear that her maids would be seduced into conspiring against her or spreading malicious gossip. She was no less concerned for her safety than for her reputation as the Virgin Queen—an image that her detractors at home and abroad regarded with skepticism and were eager to shatter.

If any man had the charm to persuade the queen to part with her virginity, it was Robert Dudley. His appointment as Master of the Horse kept him close to the queen and displayed him to great advantage. He was expert in horsemanship, horse breeding, and chivalrous combat—vigorous pursuits that Elizabeth greatly admired. He could organize pageantry and theatricals and boasted a lively wit. Tall, dark haired and dark eyed, Dudley was called "the Gypsy," partly for his looks and partly for his shiftiness. No one doubted that he would try to use his position at court to restore his family's fortunes. Both his grandfather and father had been beheaded for treason. His father, John Dudley, while serving as the power behind the throne during the last years of King Edward's reign, had engineered the succession of the ill-fated Lady Jane Grey after first arranging her marriage to Robert's younger brother Guildford—a maneuver that cost John Dudley his life when Jane was toppled by Queen Mary.

Robert Dudley's many critics believed that in courting Elizabeth he was carrying on in his father's nefarious tradition and was scheming to raise the Dudley crest to royal heights. Yet Elizabeth knew all about the misadventures of his family and seemed no less fond of him as a result. Indeed, she and Dudley had much in common. Acquaintances since childhood, they had each lost a parent by execution and

Robert Dudley, one of the queen's favorites, lifts Elizabeth into the air as they dance a galliard, whose steps were so lively that gentlemen were advised to remove their swords in advance. The queen admired Dudley's skill in dancing, riding, and jousting as much as his fine speech and his fluency in foreign languages.

had been imprisoned at the same time in the Tower. Dudley had been sentenced to death like his father, but Mary had pardoned him and allowed him to seek restitution by fighting in the French war. A shrewd judge of character, Elizabeth surely recognized that Dudley was in some measure self-seeking in his devotion to her. But everyone wanted something from the queen, and few were as delightful about it as her Master of the Horse.

Dudley with his energy and ambition offered a bracing contrast to Elizabeth's various royal suitors, foreigners who tended to seem less eager. They approached her through envoys, who haggled with her councilors over the terms of any nuptial agreement. The prince who became King Erik XIV of Sweden, for example, applied for her hand by sending his brother to London, who made quite an impression there by doling out coins to the poor and pinning hearts pierced with javelins to the coats of his servants to signal Erik's love for Elizabeth. Erik himself never made it to London, however, and the marriage talks eventually collapsed. Diplomatically, Elizabeth saw more risks than rewards in a foreign match. And personally, she seemed to prefer Englishmen to foreigners, and men of action to those who let others act for them.

Dudley had one great handicap as a suitor—he was married. But his wife was ailing, and many feared that her death might eliminate the last obstacle in his path. From the early days of her reign, Elizabeth made no secret of her affection for him. She spent hours riding with him and urged him to send to Ireland for faster horses to heighten the thrill of their outings. "I fear them much," Dudley wrote, "yet she will prove them." A few months after her coronation, the Spanish ambassador heard that she was visiting Dudley "in his chamber day and night." The ambassador heard further rumors that Dudley's wife had "a malady in one of her breasts and the Queen is only waiting for her to die to marry Lord Robert." An envoy from Archduke Charles of Austria, one of her foreign suitors, felt impelled to inquire about the queen's virtue. He heard it was still unsullied. In fact, Elizabeth was seldom if ever entirely alone with Dudley.

In the months to come, Dudley rose ever higher in her favor, much to the dismay

Elegant Elizabethans, wrapped in precious pelts that only those of high rank were legally entitled to wear, play a card game called primero for high stakes. Another pastime of the wealthy was court, or royal, tennis, an indoor sport often watched by spectators *(right)*. It was played on courts at the queen's palaces and at the estates of prominent noblemen.

of William Cecil, who hoped that she would conclude a foreign match and regarded Dudley as a dangerous rival. Cecil, in conversation with the new Spanish ambassador, went so far as to portray Dudley as a potential murderer by claiming that his wife lived in fear of being poisoned. On September 8, 1560, she was found dead of a broken neck at the bottom of the stairs in the house she was occupying in Oxfordshire.

Although an inquest ruled the death an accident, Dudley's detractors preferred to believe that he was somehow responsible. The scandal made him more controversial than ever, but Elizabeth remained fond of him and he would not give up trying for her. The following summer, he staged a water party on the Thames, conducted most likely on the royal barge, with its cloth-of-gold cushions. That night, as before, Dudley flirted openly with the queen, but this time he took the game a step further. He suggested that the Spanish ambassador, who was also a bishop, could marry them then and there. Elizabeth laughed and said she doubted that the ambassador knew enough English.

That Elizabeth still cared greatly for Dudley was made clear in 1562 when she came down with smallpox. In a lucid moment, she asked that in the event of her death, Dudley be made Lord Protector of the Realm with the huge salary of £20,000 a year, adding that as God was her witness, there had never been anything improper between them. Her recovery nullified that request, but in 1564 she named him Earl of Leicester. (Like other peers, he would be known thenceforth by his title.) By one account, she fondly tickled his neck during the ceremony as she fastened his robe of estate.

This elevation did not mean that Elizabeth had any lingering thoughts of marrying Leicester herself. Rather, it was an attempt on her part to make Dudley a suitable match for her troublesome cousin Mary. Recent events had convinced Elizabeth that unless she could restrain her cousin's ambitions by linking her with the loyal Leicester, the queen of Scots would emerge as a formidable rival for the English throne.

Following the death in 1560 of her first husband, King Francis II of France,

Worshiping the Queen's Image

In an age when women rulers had few historical role models to choose from, Queen Elizabeth and her legions of admirers drew inspiration from the fabled heroines of myth and scripture. She was linked to biblical figures such as the lawgiver Deborah and likened to the goddesses of Greece and Rome. But above all, she was celebrated as the Virgin Queen— an image Elizabeth shrewdly cultivated for political purposes. By inviting comparisons with the Virgin Mary, she enhanced her appeal in a realm where Catholic sentiment remained strong. Her refusal to take a husband became an asset rather than a liability, enabling her to preserve a pristine aura that no married queen could have maintained.

But Elizabeth was careful not to appear so remote and unworldly that the men who served her found her undesirable. She used her feminine charms skillfully at court to allay hostility and inspire devotion. Indeed, she was ardently admired by dozens of prominent men, including courtiers like Robert Dudley and Sir Walter Raleigh, as well as artists, writers, dramatists, and others who wooed her in words and images that contributed greatly to her mystique. At royal tournaments and pageants, they vied with one

"a goddess and now Queene Fitter to rule a worlde than a realme"

In a painting evoking the mythical Judgment of Paris— who had to choose between three goddesses and award the golden apple to the finest— Elizabeth stands regally above the goddesses, superior to them in beauty and dignity and holding her imperial orb like a well- deserved prize.

another for her favor and paid tribute to her in chivalrous terms that recalled the legendary devotion of the Knights of the Round Table to King Arthur and Queen Guinevere. On New Year's Day and other festive occasions, they showered her with gifts laden with symbolic meaning, such as diamond-encrusted crescent moons—emblems of Diana, the beautiful and chaste huntress-goddess—or honored her with clever and often-cryptic love poems that touted her beauty and tested her wit.

That all this passion went unrequited by the Virgin Queen in no way diminished her appeal. Pure and unattainable, she remained forever alluring in the eyes of her admirers. Even in old age, she insisted on being portrayed as a young maiden with flowing red hair, but such flattering images were not just expressions of royal vanity. England flowered during her reign, and by depicting her in eternal bloom, artists expressed their hope that this bright season of promise would never end.

"I weepe for joy to see the world decay, yet see Eliza flourishing like May."

A portrait of Elizabeth at nearly 70 shows her as an ageless beauty, holding a rainbow of promise for her people and wearing a crescent of pearls in her hair to symbolize the moon goddess Diana; ropes of pearls to signal chastity; and a dress patterned with pansies, cowslips, and honeysuckle to evoke the English springtime.

A miniature shows a young man dressed in Elizabeth's favorite pattern, black and white, and surrounded by eglantine roses, associated with the queen. Her many admirers made polite love to her by presenting her with such miniatures as well as adoring poems like the one below, attributed to Raleigh, which could be read in either direction.

Hir face	*Hir tong*	*Hir wit*
So faire	*So sweete*	*So sharpe*
First bent	*Then drew*	*Then hit*
Mine eie	*Mine eare*	*My heart*
Mine eie	*Mine eare*	*My heart*
To like	*To learne*	*To love*
Her face	*Hir tong*	*Hir wit*
Doth lead	*Doth teach*	*Doth move*
Oh face	*Oh tong*	*Oh wit*
With frownes	*With cheeke*	*With smarte*
Wrong not	*Vex not*	*Wound not*
Mine eie	*Mine eare*	*My heart*
Mine eie	*Mine eare*	*My heart*
To learne	*To knowe*	*To feare*
Hir face	*Hir tong*	*Hir wit*
Doth lead	*Doth teach*	*Doth sweare*

Mary had returned to a Scotland governed by Protestant lords who had come to power with backing from England. Their spiritual leader, John Knox, distrusted Mary on the basis of her sex as well as her religion, having argued in writing that women were "frail, impatient, feeble, and foolish creatures," unfit to rule. (Such opinions made him anathema to Elizabeth, and he was barred from England.) Protestants remained dominant in Scotland after Mary resumed the throne, but she continued to practice Catholicism. And she refused to sign a recent peace treaty with England that forbade her to display English insignia on her coat of arms—a symbol of her claim to the English throne. She and her late husband, King Francis, had once ordered dinnerware provocatively decorated with English arms.

Elizabeth feared that Mary would soon strengthen her position by remarrying, perhaps taking a second husband of royal birth from France or Spain or some other Catholic power. Nine years younger than Elizabeth, Mary was not averse to exploiting her charms and yielding to a prominent suitor. She and Elizabeth, addressing each other as "dear sister," exchanged letters concerning Mary's future and her hope that if she chose a husband pleasing to the English queen, Elizabeth might formally acknowledge Mary as her heir. It would please Elizabeth if Leicester became Mary's consort, thus eliminating the threat of a hostile marriage. Yet he himself cared little for the idea. And the queen of Scots had other plans than marriage to Elizabeth's castoff.

The match Mary made instead could hardly have been less gratifying to Elizabeth. In July 1565 the queen of Scots wed her English cousin Henry Stewart, Lord Darnley. Like Mary, Darnley was of Tudor ancestry, and the marriage thus reinforced Mary's claim to the English throne and gave any child she conceived by him a firm place in the line of succession. Mary lost interest in the dissolute Darnley shortly after she became pregnant, however, and he jealously conspired with restive Protestants to murder her Italian adviser and confidant, David Riccio. Anxious to dispel rumors that Riccio was the father of the forthcoming child, Mary then lured Darnley back to her side before giving birth to a boy, James, in June 1566.

Elizabeth was dancing at Greenwich Palace when Cecil brought her word that her cousin had produced an heir. She reportedly slumped into a chair, head in hand, and lamented to her attendants, "The Queen of Scots is lighter of a fair son, while I am but a barren stock." Yet the news left her no more inclined to try for an heir of her own. As she made clear that fall when Parliament pressed her on the issue of succession, she believed that taking a husband or naming a successor would only unsettle her realm and undermine her authority. In November, when she lectured the 60 members of Parliament on the matter, she seemed to confirm her status as a virgin queen. Those who knew her best doubted that she would ever relinquish that role.

Meanwhile, Mary's relationship with Darnley was unraveling. Soon rumors were rampant that Mary had transferred her favors to her Lord High Admiral, the earl of Bothwell. The scandal reached a fever pitch in February 1567 when Darnley was found dead after an explosion ripped through his quarters in Edinburgh. Mary's subsequent marriage to Bothwell, who was widely suspected of having arranged Darnley's death, further damaged her reputation in Scotland. Her opponents rose up, drove Bothwell into exile, and imprisoned Mary in the island castle of Loch Leven. After forcing her to abdicate, they

Mary, Queen of Scots *(left)*, shown here in 1560 in mourning for her husband, King Francis II of France, went on to wed her cousin Lord Darnley, found dead with his valet in a field near Edinburgh in 1567 after a blast hurled him from his bedchamber *(above)*. Mary's future husband, Lord Bothwell, was accused of the deed, and she was forced to abdicate. She later fled to England and became a problem for another cousin, Queen Elizabeth.

crowned her infant son king of Scotland and placed the child under Protestant guardianship.

Unfortunately for Elizabeth, Mary escaped from Loch Leven in 1568 with the aid of a man said to be in love with her and ended up in England, where she presented her cousin with a dilemma. Although Elizabeth recognized Mary as a serious rival with enduring appeal to restive Catholics, she could not bring herself to treat her kinswoman and fellow queen too harshly. Mary was placed under a kind of regal house arrest, which left her with some of the comforts of a monarch but few of the liberties. The task of guarding her was assigned to the loyal earl of Shrewsbury, whose disaffected wife later charged that he was intimate with Mary. In fact, he cared no more for Mary than for his vexing wife—known as Bess of Hardwick for the estate where she later built a splendid mansion— and longed to be free of "those two demons."

If anyone had reason to feel bedeviled by Mary, however, it was Elizabeth. Although officially a prisoner, Mary exerted influence that reached far beyond the bounds of her place of confinement. She was soon to inspire the worst domestic troubles of Elizabeth's long reign.

The seeds of rebellion sprouted in the north, far from London and the influence of the court, amid a rugged landscape dominated by magnates who clung to their old ways and resented royal intrusions. Although some northern lords like the earl of Shrewsbury had come to terms with Elizabeth, others remained hostile to the queen and to her policies, which diminished their authority and threatened their Catholic faith. They lived not in Renaissance palaces glittering with glass, of the kind some wealthy landholders in the south were erecting, but in stern medieval castles that brooded defiantly over the countryside.

Prominent among these staunch traditionalists were Thomas Percy, earl of Northumberland—whose father had been executed for supporting a Catholic revolt against Henry VIII—and Charles Neville, earl of Westmorland. They had seen their beliefs menaced and offices they considered theirs by right assigned instead to Protestant interlopers or local enemies, who were many in this feuding region.

In 1569 Northumberland and Westmorland emerged as leaders of a plot to free Mary from captivity and install her as queen in Elizabeth's place. One of their confederates,

Leonard Dacre, communicated with the Spanish ambassador in London, pledging to raise 15,000 Catholics to fight for Mary if Spain sent troops. Catholic Spain was now a greater threat to Elizabeth's regime than France, where Catholics and Protestants remained bitterly at odds. But Spanish authorities waited to see what the conspiracy amounted to before committing themselves.

Despite their bold assertions, the plotters could not be sure of raising so many troops. A great landholder like Westmorland had large numbers of loyal tenants, but to prevail against the queen's forces, he and Northumberland would need the help of other powerful lords and their dependents. They hoped for the support of England's greatest peer: Thomas Howard, duke of Norfolk. Not only was Norfolk England's only duke, the highest-ranking of the nobility, he was also the richest man in the realm. His vast holdings included the last of the great medieval liberties—an area of 600 square miles exempt from royal control. He had several splendid mansions, including Kenninghall in the Norfolk countryside; another palace in the town of Norwich replete with a tennis court, a bowling alley, and a theater; and a great house near the London Wall. When he traveled to London, 500 retainers accompanied him on horseback. He could summon an army of more than 1,200 men from among his own tenants.

But was Norfolk prepared to join a treasonous plot against the Crown? Unlike the remote counties of Northumberland and Westmorland, his domain lay only 100 miles or so northeast of London, and he and many of his tenants, while perhaps still Catholics at heart, paid lip service to the moderate Protestantism favored by Elizabeth. Norfolk attended her court, and though she sometimes scolded him, as she did when he and other lords asked her to appoint a successor, she respected his rank and showed him consideration.

On the other hand, he was proud and restless, and he resented the fact that a man of relatively low birth like Cecil had more influence with the queen than he did. Perhaps only a crown would satisfy his ambitions. A widower in his early thirties, he found the idea of marrying the queen of Scots attractive,

Proud Bess of Hardwick Hall

Bess of Hardwick, shown here in elegant dress befitting her wealth, capped a career that brought her from modest origins to noble heights by overseeing construction of Hardwick Hall, among the greatest of Elizabethan England's great houses.

Elizabeth, countess of Shrewsbury, later known as Bess of Hardwick for the great house she built there in Derbyshire *(below)*, was born in 1527 of minor gentry and rose, through four husbands and eight decades, to become the richest woman in England next to the queen. By 1567, when she married the earl of Shrewsbury, having outlived three husbands of progressively greater fortune, she was a formidable figure in her own right, shrewd, resourceful, and domineering.

The earl was much the same, and their relationship grew increasingly strained after he received custody of Mary, Queen of Scots. Bess and her husband came to think the worst of each other, and in 1583 she spread scurrilous rumors that he was involved with Mary. Queen Elizabeth herself tried to reconcile the Shrewsburys, without success. Bess separated from the earl and re-turned to the small manor she was raised in at Hardwick. Her husband died in 1590, leaving Bess enormously rich and allowing her to begin work on the house of her dreams–Hardwick Hall.

Bess realized those dreams with the help of Robert Smythson, the designer of other great Elizabethan houses. Their plan for Hardwick Hall reflected the confident mood of Elizabethan England. The return

Hardwick Hall's long gallery, extending 162 feet and richly adorned with tapestries and paintings, served as a meeting place and living room for the hostess, her family, and guests.

Embroideries such as this one—which bears the initials *ES*, for Elizabeth of Shrewsbury—were crafted by Bess and her ladies as wall hangings or as covers for cushions or stools.

of peace and prosperity after the Wars of the Roses ushered in a period known as the Great Rebuilding, when wealthy families put up gracious manors that bore no resemblance to the castles of old, which had been designed to ward off attack. Moats were no longer necessary, and windows—once limited to slits for defensive purposes—became so prominent that Hardwick Hall was said to be "more glass than wall."

Those windows were arranged with perfect symmetry, reflecting the belief that the design of a house should mirror the orderliness of society. This meant that some windows actually straddled two floors. Others were false windows concealing chimneys (the flues ran up the interior of the wall so that the exterior could accommodate more windows). All that glass made Hardwick Hall extremely cold in

winter but afforded Bess and her guests splendid views of the grounds.

Although Bess decorated her house in grand style, she kept her expenses down by furnishing some of the embroidery herself, with the help of her attendants, and using building materials almost exclusively from her own holdings—stone from her quarry, wood from her forest, and glass and iron from the works she owned. She moved into the house in 1597, but work on it continued until 1603. She died at Hardwick Hall on February 13, 1608, at the age of 80, with "the blessing of sense and memory to the last," as one eulogist put it, and with the satisfaction of having fashioned something of lasting beauty from the bitter legacy of her marriage.

Dubbed the sea dog table for the fantastic figures crouching at its base, this walnut masterpiece with tortoise feet was among Bess's treasures at Hardwick Hall.

not because he admired her (he claimed to be appalled by her conduct) but because he saw himself as a fitting king and consort for a woman who still had claim to rule Scotland and might one day rule England, presumably under his own firm guidance. That hope was not in itself necessarily treasonous. Others at court, including the queen's beloved earl of Leicester, wanted to see Mary wedded to an Englishman and considered Norfolk the best candidate. They trusted that Elizabeth, when apprised of the scheme, would sanction a match that would free Mary from captivity and tie her to the presumably trustworthy duke.

Yet Elizabeth had reason to wonder if Norfolk could really be trusted. In the summer of 1569, she got wind of his plans and gave him several chances to tell her what he was up to. She even dined with him privately to see if he would talk about it, but he held back. Finally, after learning all about the marriage scheme from a repentant Leicester, she broached the subject with Norfolk and ordered him to abandon his plans. Norfolk promised to comply, claiming that he had no need to be Mary's consort when his own revenues were nearly equal to those of all of Scotland and adding that when he was in his tennis court at Norwich, "he thought himself in a manner equal with some kings."

In truth, he remained eager to wed Mary and seemed ready to join with Northumberland and Westmorland in freeing her. The plotters thought they had Norfolk securely in their camp. His sister, after all, was married to Westmorland and firmly committed to the rebellion herself. But the duke lacked their resolve and dreaded Elizabeth's wrath. In September, fearing that he might be arrested, he abruptly left London for Kenninghall. Elizabeth assumed that his departure was the prelude to rebellion and sent a gentleman pensioner to Kenninghall to summon him to court. Norfolk had it in his power to defy this ominous summons and cast his lot with the defiant earls. Instead, he submitted to the queen and ended up a prisoner in the Tower, after first sending a message to Westmorland and Northumberland exhorting them to abort the rebellion lest it cost him his head.

Norfolk's surrender exasperated his sister. "What a simple man the Duke is," Lady Westmorland complained, "to begin a matter and not to go through with it!" In the tense weeks that followed, she urged her wavering husband and the equally anxious Northumberland to stand firm and prepare for war. Then in late October, they were forced to a decision when Elizabeth summoned them both to court. Their plans were utterly compromised, but they could not submit meekly as Norfolk had and hope to survive.

Toward midnight on November 9, supporters of the defiant earls were summoned by the eerie sound of church bells tolling backward—a carillon rung in reverse to signal the start of the uprising. The following day, the rebels headed for the town of Durham, site of a great medieval cathedral. Along the way, the earls picked up supporters, until they had almost 4,000 foot soldiers and more than 1,000 horsemen at their command. On November 14, they swept virtually unopposed into Durham and took possession of the cathedral, where they threw down the communion table that Protestants had installed to replace the old altar stone, tore up the new English Bible and prayer books, and celebrated Mass in Latin.

Then they marched south to the town of Ripon, where they appeared wearing the Crusaders' red cross on their tunics and carrying a banner displaying the five wounds of Christ—an emblem of the earlier Catholic uprising against Henry VIII. In Ripon, the earls issued a proclamation blaming "evil-disposed persons about the Queen's Majesty" for overturning "the true and Catholic religion." Those same malefactors, they added, had "abused the Queen, disordered the realm, and now lastly seek and procure the destruction of the nobility." The rebels thus portrayed their uprising as aimed not at Elizabeth but at her crafty advisers, notably Cecil, known to be a more militant Protestant than the queen and scorned as a social upstart who had wrested control of England's affairs from the ancient nobility. Although few of the nobles the rebels hoped to attract through such appeals answered their call, they forged ahead with their campaign to free Mary and defy Elizabeth, whose abuse by others they piously protested.

Mary was being held at Tutbury Castle, south of Ripon, and the earls and their forces hurriedly descended on that stronghold, only to learn as they approached that she had been moved farther south to Coventry. They did not dare follow in pursuit, because a royal army of 12,000 men was mobilizing to attack them, and the aid they had sought from Spain was nowhere in sight. Dispirited, the rebels retreated northward in

TREES FOR SOCIAL CLIMBERS

In Elizabethan England, wealth in itself was not enough to confer distinction on a family. Merchants and others who amassed fortunes were looked down upon by the social elite unless they could show that they had illustrious ancestors. Families with distinguished forebears like the Heskaiths (Heskeths) of Rufford recorded their genealogies on elaborate trees *(right)*, emblazoned with their coats of arms, considered the ultimate status symbols.

The task of verifying such genealogies and awarding families coats of arms was performed by the College of Heralds, whose members were not above accepting bribes from wealthy social climbers to approve fabricated pedigrees. "As for gentlemen," complained one Elizabethan chronicler, "they be made good cheap in England."

The term *gentleman* referred to all those above the common rank of yeoman farmers, laborers, and tradesmen. But a vast gulf separated plain gentlemen from those of the greater sort, including the five orders of the nobility: duke, marquess, earl, viscount, and baron.

No one joined the nobility unless born to it or raised to that perch by the queen, an exceptional honor that she restricted to a few favorites. Lesser gentlemen could still hope to become esquires like Robert Heskaith, Esq. *(top center)*, by obtaining coats of arms from the College of Heralds, legitimately or otherwise. And esquires could in turn hope to become knights like Sir Robert Heskaith *(lower left)*, a distinction that raised them to the highest rank below the nobility.

December. Along the way, they besieged and captured Barnard Castle, a royal stronghold, but their numbers soon diminished as men trailed off and returned home. Northumberland and Westmorland fled to Scotland, leaving Leonard Dacre to make a brief and futile stand against the queen's forces the following February, thus ending for good the rebellious stirrings in the north.

Before the winter was out, royal forces had rounded up and hanged hundreds of suspected rebels of little or no means. Those who were wealthier generally escaped death, but they paid with their fortunes or their estates. Northumberland was reclaimed from Scotland for a bounty of £2,000 and executed at York in 1572. Westmorland escaped to the Spanish Netherlands, where he died an impoverished exile. The redoubtable Lady Westmorland, whom Elizabeth could not help but admire, was spared and remained in England.

The duke of Norfolk might have enjoyed a similar reprieve, if not for his fatal longing to be king to Mary's queen. He was transferred from the Tower to house arrest in 1570, after authorities determined that his dealings with the northern rebels had stopped short of treason and he pledged to avoid any further contact with Mary. But he continued to correspond with her. And while still under house arrest, he held a covert meeting with a Catholic agent from abroad and entered into a scheme to enthrone Mary in Elizabeth's place—a plot that soon came to light.

This time there would be no mercy. A papal bull issued in 1570, excommunicating Elizabeth and absolving her Catholic subjects from allegiance to her, left English Protestants ill disposed to pardon anyone conspiring against their queen. Norfolk was tried by his peers and unanimously condemned. Elizabeth put off enacting the death warrant but came under pressure from Parliament, where members were baying for the blood not only of Norfolk but also of that "monstrous dragon," the queen of Scots, as one speaker put it. Although unwilling to act against Mary, Elizabeth finally concluded that the duke would have to die. On June 2, 1572, speaking from the scaffold where his head would be severed from his body, Norfolk proclaimed his loyalty to Elizabeth and expressed his hope that as the first man executed in the Tower during her reign, he would also be the last.

In the summer of 1578, six years after Norfolk's execution, Elizabeth set out from Greenwich on a progress that would take her to Norwich, where the duke had once resided in splendor. Since the failed uprising, her prestige and popularity had increased. Many in England, one chronicler related, were now celebrating her accession day, November 17, each year with sermons, prayers, "joyful ringing of bells, running at tilt, and festival mirth, in testimony to their affectionate love towards her." The queen heartily returned their affection. She liked to say that she was married to the people, waving her coronation ring as proof. It was this sentiment that informed her summer progresses, mingled with a precautionary urge on the part of the queen and her councilors to reward the faithful and discourage dissenters.

Elizabeth and her hundreds of courtiers and attendants usually traveled on horseback—coaches were still something of a novelty and moved with difficulty along the pitted dirt roads of the day—accompanied by a baggage train of some 300 carts loaded with supplies, each pulled by a six-horse team. At best, the train covered 12 miles in a day. The queen often stayed in private homes during progresses, which cost the owners considerably but brought them great credit. Those courtiers who were closest to her occupied the same house; others stayed in tents, inns, or neighboring houses.

Preparations for the progress to Norwich began months in advance. By July 11, when Elizabeth left Greenwich, all the houses in which she planned to stay along her route had been inspected and the area certified free from plague. The queen's purveyors moved out in advance to obtain provisions for each stop in local markets at set prices, often resented as too low by the merchants. Teams headed by gentlemen ushers leapfrogged from house to house, taking down furniture and hangings after the queen left one site and hurrying ahead to set them up at another. The queen and her council continued to conduct official business as they traveled, and the Postmaster of the Court arranged for mail pickups and deliveries along the route.

It took Elizabeth more than a month to progress northward to Norwich house by house. On August 11, she arrived at Kenninghall, the late duke's great palace in Norfolk. Her host was his eldest son and heir, Philip Howard, who would later convert to Catholicism and die a prisoner in the Tower. In 1578, however, he was eager to ingratiate himself with the queen and spent £10,000 entertaining her. From Kenninghall, the royal entourage proceeded to Norwich, with one last stop at a house where Elizabeth spent the night, then donned sumptuous clothes—the kind seen in her portraits—to honor the reception awaiting her in town.

On Saturday morning, August 16, she and her company approached the many-spired city, with its Norman castle high on a hill, its streets and markets below, and its lovely cathedral rising beside the little Wensum River. Norwich had been swelled in recent years by 6,000 Protestant refugees from the Spanish-ruled Low Countries, and the city was now home to some 16,000 people, making it second in population to London, the only place in Eng-

George Clifford, earl of Cumberland, stands ready for jousting at a tournament held annually on Elizabeth's accession day, November 17. Cumberland, who won the title of Queen's Champion, vied for royal favor with both his lance and his dazzling outfit, including star-studded hose and armor, a gem-encrusted surcoat, and Elizabeth's own glove, sewn on his hat.

land that ranked as a great city on the scale of Paris or Rome.

Townspeople had been working since June to prepare for the queen's visit. Thoroughfares were graveled or widened, muck heaps carted away, and the menacing pillory and punishment cage in the middle of town removed. House fronts were replastered, chimneys swept, and the riverbank privies cleaned up. Cows and pigs were banished from ditches and lanes. Butchers had to take their waste elsewhere. The city council borrowed £500 for expenses that included entertainment, and the waits, or city musicians, got extra pay for new uniforms.

The mayor met the queen at the outskirts of town accompanied by 60 handsome young bachelors from Norwich wearing black hose, black taffeta hats with yellow bands, and purple jackets with long sleeves embellished with silver lace. Filling out the elegant reception party were dignitaries in velvet coats, the officers of the city in scarlet and the former sheriffs in violet. Men stood by to hold back the crowds, who greeted Elizabeth with such cheers, noted one observer, that "hardly for a great time could anything be heard." The mayor gave a speech in Latin and presented the queen with a sword and a lidded, silver-gilt cup filled with £100 in gold. She said she had not come for gifts, but for the hearts of her subjects. "Princes have no need of money," she insisted, "God hath endowed us abundantly." Ever mindful of her finances, however, she passed the cup to one of her gentlemen for safekeeping and made sure that he appreciated the value of its contents, which the mayor had expressed in Latin. "Look to it," she ordered, "there is a hundredth pound."

In due course, the royal procession entered Norwich through St. Stephen's Gate, freshly painted and adorned with the queen's coat of arms, among other insignia. The smartly outfitted waits serenaded the queen, and girls on a stage demonstrated weaving and knitting for her while a boy recited a poem by way of explanation. As always in public, she listened patiently and thanked the children for their efforts. Thomas Churchyard, a poet who

produced shows for the queen in Norwich, wrote afterward that she would not allow "anything dutifully offered to pass unregarded."

The festival atmosphere continued until Friday, August 22, when Elizabeth, having knighted five deserving gentlemen at the Bishop's Palace in the morning, rode through the garlanded streets and out through the gate. Thomas Churchyard was there dressed as a water sprite with 12 boys costumed as fairies, and they danced with tambourines to amuse the queen, who laughed appreciatively. She made one last stop at the limits of Norwich, two miles farther on, where she knighted the mayor and bade farewell to the town. "I shall never forget Norwich," she declared, and rode away with tears in her eyes.

Members of her Privy Council stayed behind in Norwich, however, to take up a serious matter that belied the cheerful mood of the past week—the examination of Catholic recusants, or those who refused to attend church as the law demanded. Aided by the bishop, who furnished a list of nearly 50 offenders with information on their assets, the councilors examined the recusants and passed judgment. First-time offenders had to post bail and accept religious instruction. If they remained defiant, they could be imprisoned. There had been earlier efforts to discipline Puritans in the area, but the Privy Council concentrated on Catholics,

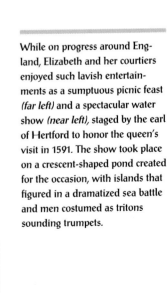

While on progress around England, Elizabeth and her courtiers enjoyed such lavish entertainments as a sumptuous picnic feast *(far left)* and a spectacular water show *(near left)*, staged by the earl of Hertford to honor the queen's visit in 1591. The show took place on a crescent-shaped pond created for the occasion, with islands that figured in a dramatized sea battle and men costumed as tritons sounding trumpets.

for it was they who stood to gain if Elizabeth was overthrown and Mary succeeded her.

"Let it not be said that our reformation tendeth to cruelty," Elizabeth once declared. But in the years following her progress to Norwich, religious tensions in her realm increased, and Spain in particular sought to exploit that situation. The queen and her councilors grew harsher toward dissenters. Some were tortured or maimed, including a few rash Puritans such as John Stubbes, a lawyer and landowner from Norfolk who in 1579 published a pamphlet denouncing the last serious foreign suitor to pay court to Elizabeth—the duke of Anjou, a French Catholic who nearly won her consent. Stubbes wrote that Elizabeth, now 45, was being led like a "lamb to the slaughter" into wedlock with a man who could have only sinister motives for marrying a woman much older than he and unlikely now to bear a child safely. Stubbes and the printer who distributed the pamphlet each had his right hand chopped off in punishment. Moments after he sustained the blow, Stubbes proclaimed his loyalty by doffing his cap with his left hand and crying, "God save the Queen!"

Worse treatment awaited Catholics who went abroad to study as priests and returned furtively to England, where they risked being hanged, drawn, and quartered as traitors. Increasingly, Elizabeth and her councilors saw themselves as involved in an irregular war against a shadowy opposition that included English Catholics and their foreign backers, with Spain acting as chief instigator. And nothing did more to comfort and inspire that opposition, the queen's advisers reasoned, than the knowledge that Mary was still alive, ready when called upon to ascend the English throne.

One man in particular kept a sharp eye on Mary and hoped to bring her down— Sir Francis Walsingham, a strict Protestant who succeeded Cecil as Elizabeth's principal secretary in 1573. Among other duties, he had the task of protecting her from plots against her life. Walsingham was small,

The grim-visaged Sir Francis Walsingham, who monitored plots against Elizabeth as her principal secretary, kept a sharp eye on Mary, Queen of Scots, and her Catholic backers at home and abroad. "There is less danger in fearing too much than too little," he once remarked, and his worst fears about Mary were ultimately confirmed.

dark, and always dressed in black. Elizabeth called him her "Moor" and put up with his blunt and sometimes unwelcome advice because she knew he was fiercely devoted to her welfare. "I wish God's glory and next the Queen's safety," Walsingham once remarked. And he was convinced that the queen would never be safe from Mary "so long as that devilish woman lives."

To protect Elizabeth and her interests, Walsingham relied on a remarkable intelligence network paid for with secret treasury funds. His far-flung agents infiltrated embassies and ports at home and abroad, spying on ship and troop movements as well as contacts between foreign officials and English malcontents. His men also watched over the household of Mary Stuart.

In 1583 Walsingham thwarted a serious international conspiracy to overthrow Elizabeth in favor of Mary. That November, after months of surveillance, he hauled in Francis Throckmorton, a Catholic in close contact with Mary, and extracted from him under torture an admission that he had plotted against the Crown with the Spanish ambassador, Bernardino de Mendoza, among other foreigners. The plot, conceived with Mary's knowledge, called for a two-pronged invasion of England and Scotland, combined with a domestic uprising. Some of the conspirators escaped to the Continent, but others were executed along with Throckmorton. Mendoza, expelled from England, warned in parting that since his efforts as a "minister of peace" had failed to please Elizabeth, he must try in the future to "satisfy her in war."

Elizabeth once again refused to prosecute Mary, but she recognized the threat her cousin posed at a time when Spain was indeed drifting toward war with England and inclined to support any credible plot against the Crown. Walsingham and others on the Privy Council were so intent on holding Mary responsible for any further conspiracies that in 1584 they composed and circulated copies of an oath called the Bond of Association, which pledged those who signed it to protect the queen and kill

anyone who plotted against her life or stood to benefit from such a plot—a plain reference to Mary.

Thousands signed this drastic oath, which alarmed Elizabeth because it amounted to a lynch law and meant that Mary's son James in Scotland might suffer because he stood to benefit indirectly by Elizabeth's death. Parliament addressed her concerns in 1585 by passing an act that called for commissioners to investigate plotters and pass judgment, and exempted from punishment those who might gain by the plot but had no knowledge of it. The same act confirmed that Mary would have to pay with her life, however, if privy to any future conspiracy.

For Mary, the risks of encouraging her supporters had never been greater. Shrewsbury had been succeeded as her overseer by a stern Puritan, Sir Amias Paulet, who placed her under strict confinement and clamped down on her secret correspondence. Mary eventually resumed that correspondence, but only through the devious efforts of an English Catholic named Gilbert Gifford, whom Walsingham had induced to betray her. Mary's coded letters were smuggled out in beer kegs by a local brewer who played both sides, accepting payment from Mary and from Walsingham. The brewer then passed her letters on to Gifford, who slipped them to Walsingham to be deciphered and copied before Gifford completed the delivery. Secret messages to Mary followed the same path in reverse.

Among the letters intercepted in this fashion was one Mary wrote in May 1586 to Mendoza, now the Spanish ambassador in Paris, welcoming a proposed invasion of England on her behalf. By that time, Mendoza had made contact with English Catholics who were prepared to assassinate Elizabeth as the first blow in an uprising and invasion that would free Mary to assume the English throne. The leader of the would-be assassins was one Anthony Babington, who had come under Mary's spell while serving as a page in Shrewsbury's household and had resolved to rescue her. Babington informed Mary of his intentions by letter in

July, and Walsingham snared that secret message along with Mary's incriminating reply, approving the assassination attempt. Once in custody, Babington and his confederates promptly confessed. After being tried and condemned, they were led off to the gallows in September. Babington and several others received the full punishment specified for traitors of common rank, meaning that they were drawn, or disemboweled, before they died by hanging, and their bodies were then quartered.

Mary's fate was sealed. In late October a special commission of lords, councilors, and judges unanimously found her guilty of "encompassing" the queen's murder, and shortly thereafter Parliament concurred and asked for Mary's execution. The death warrant required Elizabeth's signature, however, and she delayed for months in a state of high anxiety. She dreaded condemning a kindred queen and may well have been haunted by thoughts of the beheading that awaited Mary—the same end Elizabeth's mother had met and that she herself had faced while imprisoned in the Tower. More than that, she feared destroying her reputation. What would people think, she asked, when it appeared that "for the safety of her life, a maiden queen could be content to spill the blood even of her own kinswoman?"

On February 1, 1587, she finally signed the death warrant and entrusted it to William Davison, one of her lesser secretaries. Then in a desperate effort to avoid an execution and escape public responsibility, she had Davison write to Sir Amias Paulet, asking him to kill Mary under the terms of the Bond of Association. Paulet refused, eloquently: "God forbid that I should make so foul a shipwreck of my conscience or leave so great a blot to my poor posterity to shed blood without law or warrant."

When word reached Eliza-

Mary, Queen of Scots, prepares to die on February 8, 1587, by placing her head on the block at Fotheringhay, her last place of detention, while her maidservants weep and a smoking bonfire signals her death. Having spent nearly half of her 44 years in confinement, sustained by a fervent Catholicism, Mary went to her death wearing her rosary *(left)* and reciting in Latin from her prayer book: "Into your hands, O Lord, do I commend my soul!"

beth that Mary had been beheaded on the morning of February 8, the queen wildly denounced her councilors for executing the warrant without further orders from her. (In fact, she had made it plain to them that she wanted as little to do with Mary's death as possible.) In a blind fury, she singled out Davison as a scapegoat and had him imprisoned in the Tower, threatening to have him hanged. Few at court had ever seen her in a worse state, but like her other tempests, this one subsided without causing grievous harm. Davison was later freed and faded into obscurity.

After the storm was over, Elizabeth revived, and she remained a continuing source of hope and inspiration to her people. Their nation was still beset by challenges, and dark days lay ahead, but they looked to their resilient queen to brighten their path and to guide them through.

Greate · Yarmowthe

The North

Life in the English Countryside

The many progresses Queen Elizabeth made from London took her into the English countryside, where fully three-quarters of her subjects lived. Almost 650 towns and 10,000 villages dotted the rural landscape, most of them in fertile farming and fishing areas in the southern part of the country.

Like London society, rural residents followed a prescribed social order. Nobles, knights, and landed gentlemen were at the top, then came the middle-class group comprising merchants and businessmen. Under that were craftsmen or farmers who owned at least part of the land they worked. Lower still were domestic servants and day laborers, and beggars and vagrants made up society's bottom rung.

Rural life centered around work, the church, and the local alehouses. Most country people lived in a town or village, even farmers: Every day, they walked from their homes to work in the fields. Only in hilly or wooded areas did families live on isolated farms. Sundays were days of rest and worship, and on holy days the church put on festivals that brought all the townspeople together.

Fields and grazing lands surround the walled town of Great Yarmouth on England's coast. Also home to mariners and fishermen, the town hosted the annual Yarmouth Fishing Fair, where, according to a book published in 1614, men went "aboute the takinge, sellinge, and buying of herrings."

A Family at Work

It took both husband and wife working to make a comfortable living in 16th-century rural England. The husband, the acknowledged head of the family, likely worked as a farmer or tradesman, while the wife ran the household of children, servants, and apprentices. Although the gentry tended to marry at a younger age, most men and women waited until about age 26 or 27 to wed, when the men had finished any apprenticeships they might be pursuing and could afford to set up a household. The typical family had anywhere from three to five children, although wealthy families might have as many as 12. Once in their teens, children left home to work as farm hands, domestic servants, or apprentices.

Farming took place under the traditional open-field system, whereby villages and towns divided the arable land—usually owned by a wealthy landlord—into three large fields. Farmers leased and cultivated strips of land scattered throughout those fields. Enclosure, the practice by landlords of consolidating and fencing their land that had begun in the 15th century, continued, and although it resulted in a more efficient farming system, it put many farm laborers out of work.

Besides agriculture and the trades that supported it, English countrymen engaged in a variety of other jobs, including making salt from seawater, shipbuilding, construction, fishing, mining, and basic manufacturing such as tanning and shoemaking. Many men and women also worked in their homes in some aspect of the wool and cloth trade, such as spinning, weaving, or dyeing fabrics.

Under the watchful eye of an overseer, men and women cut and stack sheaves of grain. By act of Parliament, justices of the peace had the authority to order craftsmen and other able-bodied people, when needed, out to work in the field.

Women took care of the house and prepared the meals, and they bought goods for the household at market *(left).* Homes often had floors of packed dirt or stone, and only the well-to-do had sanitary facilities other than chamber pots, which were emptied into public cesspools or gutters in town.

A shepherd and a cowherd greet each other in the fields outside of town. Villagers grazed their animals in the common pastures and woodlands and in cultivated fields after the harvest.

Rising waters sweep away children, adults, and livestock in this depiction of a flood. Floods and droughts were a constant fear for many country dwellers, whose livelihoods—and very survival—could be threatened by the weather.

Amusements and Festivities

After laboring long and hard, countryfolk looked forward to the many celebrations hosted throughout the year by their parish church. There were solemn religious processions and services as well as a variety of amusements that included church-ales, where food and drink were sold to raise funds for the parish. The wealthiest citizens paid a large portion of the costs, and even opened their homes to the townspeople at harvesttime and again during Christmas.

Most holidays combined the religious and the secular. During the Christmas season, Elizabethans decorated their homes with the pagan symbols of holly and ivy, watched religious plays, held parties, played cards and board games, passed the wassail bowl, and sang carols. At Shrovetide—observed during the three days before Ash Wednesday—celebrants ate foods that would be forbidden during Lent,

and men took part in street sports such as football, footraces, and cockfights. The clergy did not sponsor those contests, however, and in 1570 a disapproving Protestant preacher described one such raucous occasion as "a day of great gluttony, surfeiting and drunkenness."

The agricultural year began with ceremonies of Plough Monday, the first day of the plowing season in late winter. This was followed by a nod to the beginning of summer, or May Day. On this day, citizens

An engraving depicts a lively game of football, a popular sport the men played on holidays and Sundays, their days of leisure. Many towns banned the playing of the game, which one writer described as "nothing but beastly fury and extreme violence, whereof procedeth hurt."

A swimmer demonstrates how "to swimme with his hands together," in the words of Everard Digby in his 1595 book, *De Arte Natandi* (The Art of Swimming). Englishmen participated in all kinds of outdoor sports, including fishing, which was popular among all classes of society and served as a source of both recreation and food.

decorated their homes with greenery and began a season of festivals that could stretch into July, depending on when the community decided to put on their summer games. Such festivities could include Maypoles, May queens, plays, and dancing. The English observed midsummer with bonfires, "Whose wholesome heat, purging the air, consumes / The earth's unwholesome vapours, fogs, and fumes." The ritual was thought to guard crops and people from bad weather and disease.

The first of August marked the formal start to the harvest season and the conclusion of the agricultural year. Harvest suppers were held, harvest queens were crowned, and as a German traveler observed, "Their last load of corn they crown with flowers, having besides an image richly dressed, by which perhaps they would signify Ceres."

Eventually, Protestant religious reforms and concern for public order forced officials to sharply curtail the number of holiday celebrations. Protestant clergy preached against dancing and other merrymaking on Sundays, and the 95 feast days were reduced to 27. "And with them," proclaimed a Protestant clergyman, "the superfluous number of idle wakes, guilds, fraternities, church-ales ... with the heathenish rioting at brideales, are well diminished and laid aside."

In a small town just outside London, townsfolk celebrate a wedding on the green in front of the market hall. This painting from about 1570 shows tables set up inside the hall in preparation for a feast, while a group of Flemish men and women dressed all in black watch the festivities from under a tree *(right)*.

S. Dunston inde caft

Leadne Hall   S. Hellen   S. Andrew   Alhallowes

Lion Kay

BRIDGE

S. Mary Oueris

CHAPTER TWO

London, City of Opportunity

A gruesome display of traitors' heads *(bottom right)* tops the entrance to London Bridge, which spans the Thames River and links the south bank to the heart of the English capital *(background)*. The city, wrote a Swiss visitor, was "so superior to other English towns that London is not said to be in England, but rather England to be in London."

The citizens of London were enjoying an unexpected holiday on February 8, 1587, the day an 11-year-old named David Baker arrived there from his home in south Wales. Bells rang festively, gunshots filled the air, and bonfires crackled in every part of the city late into the evening as Protestant Londoners celebrated the good news: Queen Elizabeth's Catholic cousin, Mary, Queen of Scots, had been beheaded. Along the Thames River, flames from the fires illuminated the tall, elegant houses and shops atop London Bridge, a broad stone structure threaded by a narrow roadway. At one end of the bridge, the flickering glow revealed the grotesque visages of some 30 disembodied heads, rotting on poles over the gatehouse—a grisly warning of the fate awaiting anyone found guilty of treason.

Young Baker may not have known what to make of the celebration awaiting him in London, for he was a product of the religious confusion of his era. His father, a justice of the peace, had long maintained an inner allegiance to Catholicism, even as he outwardly conformed as a Protestant. As time went on, however, the elder Baker "came to lose all sense of Catholic religion," according to his son, "and nothing troubled his mind either one way or other." Not surprisingly,

David and his 12 older siblings grew up with no deep religious convictions. So on this tumultuous winter evening in 1587, he may well have been more concerned with his own immediate future than with Mary's fate.

Baker had been sent to further his education in England's bustling capital, and in the years to follow, he would come to know the sights, sounds, and smells of its crowded avenues in all their glory and misery. The greatest of those thoroughfares, as he and other newcomers soon discovered, was the Thames River, the city's main artery for travel, commerce, and sightseeing. Visitors often commented on the beautiful white swans that floated gracefully on its waters. The elegant birds were protected by city officials, who charged anyone who killed one with a sizable fine. Floating alongside the swans were the small upholstered boats known as wherries, some 2,000 of which plied the river. Watermen propelled their wherries with oars as they ferried passengers upstream or down, signaled by cries of "Eastward ho!" or "Westward ho!" Larger craft, crammed with people or cargo, were powered by oar or sail. Vessels discharged passengers along the riverbanks, where they engaged rooms at various taverns and inns and enjoyed such fare as meat pies or roasts, along with fruit tarts, cheese, and wine.

Those traveling upstream from London Bridge could see to their left the lively if disreputable district known as Southwark, the site of prisons, bear and bull pits, and theaters. To their right on the north bank lay the city proper, dominated by St. Paul's Cathedral. Farther upstream, courtiers disembarked from boats onto private stairways, which led to magnificent homes along the fashionable road known as the Strand. Now occupied by the nobility and other well-to-do Londoners, many of the mansions had once been the property of Catholic prelates. The queen's own palace of Whitehall, nearby, had been confiscated from the archbishop of York and rebuilt by her father to become the largest royal residence in Europe.

Young David Baker no doubt admired the splendid view of London from the Thames, but he could not begin to savor the city without venturing down its bustling streets. There shoppers rubbed elbows with beggars and pickpockets, and vendors raised tempting cries of "Pies, meat pies, sir!" while other sellers offered oysters, bread, oranges, cheese, cakes, puddings—or fresh water, transported underground to London in lead conduits and doled out for a fee from tall wooden tankards hauled by water carriers. No street offered more to delight the eye or the palate than Cheapside, the city's broadest avenue, located north of London Bridge

Fishmongers display their offerings on shop boards in front of their houses on a London street named for their trade. This drawing illustrated a report concerning market violators such as regraters, who bought goods and then resold them at a higher price in the same market or nearby. To enforce economic statutes, the Crown relied on informers.

Believing that bad air caused disease, Elizabethans of means carried pomanders *(below)* to ward off the pungent odors caused by fouled streets and infrequent bathing. Pomanders were filled with a mixture of cinnamon, cloves, musk, and other aromatic agents and could be worn on a necklace or suspended from a belt and held to the nose when needed.

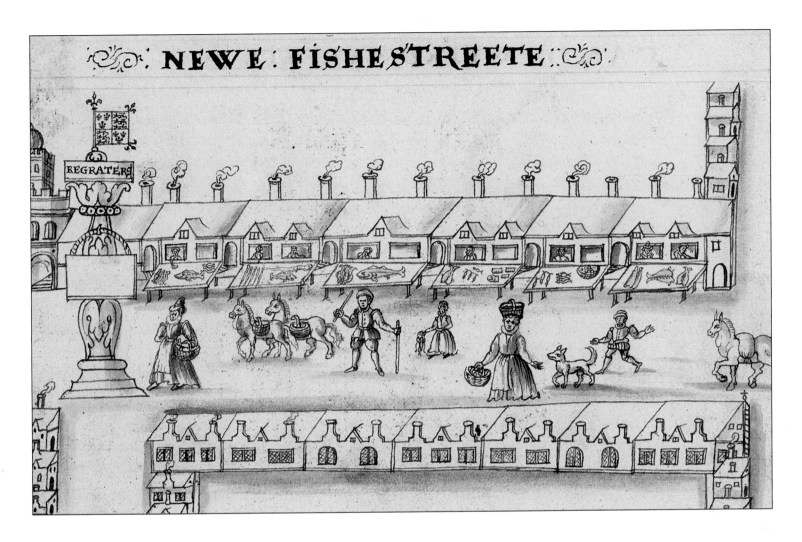

NEWE · FISHESTREETE

REGRATERS

and running southeast to northwest through the heart of the city. Cheapside was filled with stalls sheltered by canopies and stocked with a tempting array of local goods as well as such exotic imports as live peacocks and apes for the gardens and menageries of the wealthy.

Cheapside also featured sumptuous shops and homes, particularly those in its fancy Goldsmiths' Row. Other places hosted their own less exalted trades. Butchers gathered in St. Nicholas Shambles to the northwest, vendors of old clothes congregated on Houndsditch to the northeast, and printers mingled with tavern keepers and puppeteers on Fleet Street, west of St. Paul's Cathedral. Other avenues such as Milk Street, Bread Street, and

New Fish Street offered exactly what their names implied.

On narrow lanes off the main avenues could be found the cramped homes of the city's poor laborers, who often threw household waste just outside their doors. With passersby contributing to the stench, the foulest of these back streets earned names such as Pissing Alley and Stinking Lane. The threat of epidemics in such conditions was one of many hazards Londoners faced, along with the risk of fire and the fear of crime that prompted people out at night to hire attendants with torches to discourage assailants lurking in the shadows.

But none of these dangers kept eager youngsters such as David Baker or their ambitious elders from flocking to London in droves during Elizabeth's reign. By 1587 its population had swelled to well over 100,000, making it one of the largest cities in Europe and by far the biggest town in England. Fearing rampant disease and disorder, Queen Elizabeth had issued a proclamation seven years earlier banning the construction of any new houses within three miles of the city's gates, prohibiting additional families from moving into houses already occupied, and requiring lodgers who had come to London within the past seven years to leave. Her edict proved unenforceable, and the great influx continued. London was not only England's political and judicial hub but also its main port and marketplace. Lawyers and charlatans, musicians and playwrights, society gentlemen in conspicuous finery and Jesuit priests in disguise all made their way to London for the same reason young Baker did: to exploit the city's unrivaled opportunities.

In an early-17th-century engraving, sailing vessels and oar-driven boats ply the waters west of London Bridge *(far right)* along the city's busiest and most easily negotiated thoroughfare, the Thames River. Quays line its northern edge, offering access to London's crowded streets *(top)*.

St. Paul's Cathedral dominates the western side of the city *(top left)*, its height still impressive despite the loss of its spire to lightning in 1561. Directly across the river, in the rowdy suburb of Southwark, lie the Globe Theatre and the Bear Garden, which was named for its bearbaiting spectacles *(bottom left)*.

THAMESIS

The Bear Gardne

The Globe

In Baker's case, opportunity took the form of a benevolent institution called Christ's Hospital, chartered by Elizabeth's brother, King Edward, as an orphanage and charity school for the poor. Most of its charges were educated for a trade, but exceptional wards joined fee-paying students such as Baker to learn proper English (most people in Baker's homeland spoke Welsh) and to acquire the classical education they needed to enter the university. Despite the presence of such fee-paying boarders, Christ's Hospital remained essentially a charitable institution. Residents wore blue uniforms because blue dye was cheap. Boys sported a long blue coat and yellow stockings, the color chosen because it supposedly discouraged lice. Girls wore dresses of the same blue color over yellow petticoats and were housed separately from the boys.

Like the other boys preparing for the university, Baker became well versed in Latin, still considered the gateway to all higher knowledge. He learned to write it and speak it through such exercises as translating segments of the English Bible favored by Protestants into Latin and memorizing long passages of classical and biblical wisdom. Yet schooling was as much about learning lessons of morality and religion as it was about learning Latin.

At mealtimes, Baker and other Christ's Hospital students filed

into the dining hall where, before being seated, one of them read a chapter from the English Bible under the watchful eyes of the headmaster and -mistress. Only after the reading could students eat. Christ's Hospital regularly served its charges bread, meat, butter, cheese, and beer, which was considered better for the mind and the body than milk. (In the opinion of one authority, milk rendered children "stupid and vacant," like the animals from which it came.) Other religious expressions included the singing of a hymn as the students left the classroom at the end of the day and kneeling at bedtime while one of the students read prayers—activities the adult Baker would characterize as a "poor kind of devotion."

Sundays and holy days brought a more rigorous expression of the Protestant faith, when twice a day Baker and his fellows lined up behind the headmaster and -mistress and marched off to Christ Church. They listened attentively to the preacher's words, some scribbling notes that would be reviewed later by their instructor. Such sermons were filled with stern lessons and warnings for those who sinned, particularly by straying into heresy.

Despite such determined efforts to set young Baker on a straight path, he later took a turn abhorrent to his Protestant teachers and preachers. After studying at Oxford and reading law, he converted to Catholicism and left England to become a Benedictine monk and later an ordained priest. As Augustine Baker, he composed some 60 treatises and devoted himself to prayer and contemplation for up to six hours a day. Late in his life, Father Baker wrote of his upbringing and conversion, looking back with sadness and dismay on the fiery celebration of Mary's execution that lighted up the great city of London on the evening he arrived there as a boy—a display of "unworthy joy," as he put it, "odious to all truly pious hearts."

In a busy Tudor schoolroom, a teacher punishes a boy with a rod of birch twigs *(left)* while fellow students continue their lessons. Some pupils in the corner are learning their ABCs with the aid of hornbooks like the one at right, named for the layer of animal horn that protected the sheet bearing the letters.

Christ's Hospital was one of several institutions in London that tried with mixed results to mold the beliefs and behavior of the young and the needy. Those who supported such institutions were motivated in part by generous impulses, but also by a desire to maintain social order. Well-to-do Elizabethans worried about rising poverty and the crime that accompanied it. They hoped places such as Christ's Hospital could turn poor children into useful members of society. But most of the poor were well beyond school age and more likely to be offered punishment than a helping hand.

Amid the fast-growing population of poor were legions of so-called masterless men and women, who had no regular occupation, no employer, and no fixed abode. Many were the sons and daughters of freeholders, or small farmers, who had lost their land and could no longer support their families. Others were seasonal agricultural workers, discharged soldiers and sailors, and dismissed servants. Traveling to London in search of work, they soon discovered that there were not nearly enough jobs to go around and so joined the swelling ranks of vagrants, who often turned to theft, prostitution, or begging to get money.

Begging, in fact, could be more lucrative than honest labor, but like thievery and prostitution, it ranked as a punishable offense. Among other laws governing vagrancy, it was considered a crime for "sturdy," or able-bodied, vagrants to beg. If London beggars wanted to avoid punishment, they had to be genuinely sick or crippled—or at least make a convincing show of it. Such was the stratagem of a sturdy rogue named Nicholas Jennings, who ran afoul of authorities early in Elizabeth's reign.

One autumn morning in 1566, Thomas Harman, a writer from Kent visiting London, heard noises in the courtyard of his inn. He stepped outside and discovered a man whose countenance he described as "loathsome and horrible" begging alms from some women. The stranger wore a loose jacket of patched leather and a pair of hose so dirty that it looked "as though he had wallowed in the mire," Harman wrote. He had a "filthy foul cloth" wrapped around his head, exposing only part of his face, which was smeared with fresh blood. Harman asked the man what ailed him and how he had arrived at this pitiful condition. "I have the grievous and painful disease called the falling sickness," the beggar replied, referring to epilepsy. "I fell down on the backside here in the foul lane hard by the waterside;

Passing the Poor Laws

The men who met in the parliamentary session of 1571 were alarmed: Poverty was rising and vagrancy with it. Vagrants—individuals without regular income, often traveling from place to place—were seen as a threat to social order, and the government considered most of them to be idlers who chose to be poor.

Earlier parliaments had restricted begging, ordered that vagrants be whipped and sent back to their home parishes, seized child vagrants and placed them into apprenticeships, and even permitted the enslavement of able-bodied beggars. But not many Englishmen wanted to become slave masters, and that statute was repealed. In 1572 a new vagrancy statute was enacted, stiffening penalties and bringing an array of marginal professions within the scope of the law. Palm readers, wizards, unlicensed healers, tinkers, and even minstrels were now defined as vagrants, liable to be whipped and burned on the ear for a first offense and hanged for a second, unless they quickly found masters. Four years later, authorities ordered houses of correction modeled on London's Bridewell to be built throughout England for the willfully idle.

Yet the government also admitted that some poor were "deserving." A 1570 census taken in Norwich had shown that a large percentage of the town's indigents were working families. After debate, Parliament took the historic step in 1572 of enacting a national system of personal taxation to finance weekly doles to poor householders. In 1576 it ordered towns to give the unemployed raw materials and buy back their finished products.

Rioting, crime, and even starvation from a series of meager harvests in the 1590s prompted more legislation. But by then a novel solution to the age-old problem of poverty was on the horizon: shipping the "ragged rabblement" to the New World.

A well-dressed man reaches into his purse to aid a wayside beggar covered with sores. Many Elizabethans ignored a 1598 law that made cadging leftovers from neighbors the only legal form of begging.

The Dudley crest—a bear and staff—adorns a silver badge, one of 13 that Elizabeth gave to residents of an alms-house founded by Robert Dudley. Many towns, parishes, and guilds had such homes for the elderly poor.

A seal and signatures lend authenticity to a forged passport *(above)*—a document vagrants could buy in London for a few pence. By law, many poor travelers had to carry official papers stating destination and reason for the journey. The papers protected their holders from the whippings and hangings prescribed for vagrants *(left)* and allowed them to seek aid in the communities through which they passed.

and there I lay almost all night, and have bled almost all the blood out in my body."

Offered a bowl of water to clean himself up, the beggar refused. "If I should wash myself," he explained, "I should fall to bleeding afresh again." Suspicious, Harman pressed the beggar for particulars. He gave his name as Nicholas Jennings and claimed that he had spent a year and a half in Bedlam, or Bethlehem Hospital, London's notorious institution for the deranged. Poor inmates there received little treatment except to be regularly beaten, while Londoners seeking entertainment came to watch the antics of the lunatics. To test Jennings's veracity, Harman asked him to identify Bedlam's keeper. "John Smith," replied Jennings, using an all too common English name.

Harman sent Jennings on his way, but his investigation had just begun. Unfortunately for Jennings, Harman was a nemesis of unscrupulous beggars, appealing to the public by exposing in writing the ruses of the vagrants who sought charity by feigning epilepsy, paralysis, or madness or pretending to be lame, blind, deaf, or dumb.

An inquiry at Bedlam uncovered the fact that no one named John Smith had ever been keeper there nor had anyone fitting Nicholas Jennings's description been an inmate there. Suspicions confirmed, Harman sent a note to his printer, William Griffith, asking for help in tracking down the beggar. As Harman later recounted, Griffith sent out two boys, who soon caught up with Jennings and followed him into a back lane, where he "renewed his face again with fresh blood, which he carried about him in a bladder."

With clear evidence of Jennings's duplicity, Griffith himself followed the beggar across the Thames to Newington, a rough parish south of London. There the printer alerted a constable, who arrested the beggar and planned to clap him into a holding cage on the street overnight. Such cages, used

Two wealthy men dine with high-class prostitutes, one of whom hopes to earn a bit extra by dipping into her client's purse *(center)*. London's thriving sex industry supported more than 100 bawdyhouses. Those located on the south bank of the Thames put up signs facing the river to attract potential clients traveling by boat.

for the temporary confinement of petty criminals, were typically dank cells, furnished only with straw for bedding. It promised to be a cold evening, and Griffith suggested that the constable instead take Jennings home for the night and let the beggar pay for his more comfortable lodgings. "I know well his gains hath been great today," Griffith remarked, "and your house is a sufficient prison for the time."

At the constable's house, Griffith and the officer forced their prisoner to clean up and stripped him of his rags, in the process uncovering several hidden purses containing a substantial amount of money. They then allowed the thirsty beggar three quarts of strong beer. The officer soon went out on another case, leaving his charge in the care of his wife and servants. Not long afterward, Jennings pleaded with the "goodwife" to allow him to go out in the backyard to "make water, and exonerate his paunch." Believing that the young man would never leave the grounds unclothed, the woman unlatched the door so he could go outside to relieve himself. To her astonishment, Jennings ran off, "as naked as ever he was born." He had escaped the law this time, but his next encounter with it would not end so well.

Two months after his original meeting with Jennings, printer Griffith spotted the fake epileptic using a new ruse. Well dressed in a black coat, expensive linen shirt, and fresh hose, he was posing as a hatmaker short of funds. "If I could get money to pay for my lodging this night, I would seek work tomorrow amongst the hatters," he promised. Jennings evidently believed that no constable would bother a beggar who bore so little resemblance to a vagrant. Indeed, he was prospering as a charlatan. Griffith later discovered that Jennings lived with his wife in a London suburb in a "pretty house, well stuffed, with a fair iron table, and a fair cupboard garnished with pewter." The printer had the beggar arrested and clapped into the pillory in Cheapside. After languishing there for a some time in full view of passersby, Jennings was released from the pillory and whipped through the streets to a house of correction, where he would be "rehabilitated."

Other tricksters whose frauds were discovered were similarly scourged in public, among them an imaginative swindler named Judith Phillips, who exploited the superstitions of Londoners as a so-called cunning woman—someone who claimed such magical powers as the ability to locate hidden objects, foretell the future, heal the sick with charms, or recruit the goodwill of the queen of the fairies. Judith Phillips tried one trick too many when she approached an elderly London widow named Mascall with a letter of introduction, purportedly from a friend, advising the widow to "make much of Judith," who could

Cunning woman Judith Phillips rides a bridled client as part of a supposed ritual for summoning the queen of the fairies to help find buried treasure. Phillips and other charlatans played on Elizabethan superstitions in order to rob people of their valuables.

do her "great good." Intrigued, the widow invited the cunning woman into her home and marveled as Phillips divulged details about her personal life by reading her palm. Having convinced Mascall of her powers, Phillips laid her trap. "There is money hid in your house," she proclaimed dramatically. The only way to draw this treasure out, she informed the widow, was to lure it from hiding with gold.

Eagerly, the widow collected her gold coins and gold jewelry and gave them to Phillips, who, after a bit of hocus-pocus, seemingly returned the precious items to the owner in a yarn-wrapped bundle, instructing her to put the package aside without looking at it for three days—by which time the gold would have miraculously drawn the hidden treasure to its side by virtue

of some occult power of attraction. Soon after the cunning woman left, the widow returned to her senses and unwrapped the bundle, which contained nothing but stones. Mascall promptly sent for the authorities, and Phillips was arrested when she greedily returned to the widow's house the following day, hoping to obtain additional goods. When questioned, Phillips confessed that she and an unsuccessful suitor of the widow's had conspired to rob the woman. A friend of the suitor's had forged the letter of introduction and supplied Phillips with enough facts about their intended victim to make her believe in the cunning woman's power. Phillips, meanwhile, had wrapped up the stones in preparation for the switch. Found guilty of the crime of cozening, or deceit, Phillips, like Jennings, was whipped through the streets of London.

However mortifying, such punishment at least had the advantage of being quick. What offenders feared more were long terms of confinement, whether at one of London's dismal prisons or at Bridewell, London's hulking house of correction located at the edge of the Thames, where Jennings was sent. Once a Tudor palace, Bridewell had been transformed in the 1550s into London's first house of correction, "for the poor and idle persons of the city," including rogues like Jennings who were considered ripe for rehabilitation. All were assigned tasks so that they might come out better and make an honest living. Not many of the frauds, petty thieves, and prostitutes consigned to Bridewell were reformed by the drudgery they performed, however, and some plied their old trades there, teaching the wrong lessons to impressionable young inmates whose only crime was having no occupation.

Upon entering Bridewell, Nicholas Jennings was probably assigned to work under one of the taskmasters. Perhaps he was made to pace the treadmill hour upon hour, grinding grain. If he was luckier, he labored at a less onerous job, such as making bedticking, nails, or wire. Whatever his assigned task, Jennings was not likely to balk or malinger, since prisoners often received beatings as punishment. Bridewell was popular with many law-abiding Londoners, who were pleased that unsavory

A woodcut in Thomas Harman's book exposing vagrants shows Nicholas Jennings as an "upright man," or vagabond leader *(below, left)*, and as a "counterfeit crank" feigning epilepsy *(right)*. Some fake epileptics used soap to make their mouths froth.

characters were being swept from the streets and hoped that they would emerge from confinement there suitably chastened, if not actually reformed. At one point, it became fashionable to attend the whippings of prostitutes there. London's Bridewell served as the model throughout England for other houses of correction, referred to as "bridewells."

But not everyone approved. One critic denounced Bridewell's summary arrest and imprisonment of vagrants as a violation of the Magna Carta. That royal charter, issued in the 13th century at the insistence of the English barons, promised that "no freeman shall be taken or imprisoned . . . except by the lawful judgment of his peers or the law of the land." Others on the outside disapproved of Bridewell and its overseers for more selfish reasons. Some audacious young men went so far as to mount an assault on the house of correction to free their favorite prostitutes.

Corruption plagued Bridewell. Some treasurers stole money; others filched goods. Around 1600 it was discovered that the man who had contracted to run the treadmill was using it to grind grain not for various London institutions (as stipulated by ordinance) but for his brewhouse. A few years later, four Londoners took over the management of the house of correction and proceeded to turn it upside down. Many vagrants were released and their rooms let out to rent, while a number of those who remained were left to starve. Still at work, however, were the prostitutes. They plied

RIDING THE STANG

Elizabethans could be as outraged by a social misdemeanor as by a legal one, leading to some colorful punishments. In the composite scene below, a passer-by spies a wife rapping her husband with a shoe for pouring a beer while minding the baby *(left)*.

A report to neighbors leads to a ritual known as "riding the stang" or "riding skimmington" *(right)*, intended to shame the man for allowing his wife to master him. The husband, or someone impersonating him, is paraded through the streets atop a pole—a stang—usually to the accompaniment of bells, pipes, pots, and pans. Here the rider himself plays a pipe, suggesting he may indeed be a stand-in for the henpecked husband—a skimmington.

their trade in the quarters of one of the managers, most likely turning some or all of the proceeds over to the gang now administering Bridewell. Civic authorities could not let corruption on this scale go entirely unchallenged, however. The managers lost their contract, but they escaped any harsher penalty. Though the managers had abused their charge, they had committed no clear crime under English law. Punishment was saved for malefactors such as Nicholas Jennings, who after doing his sentence, was released from Bridewell with the admonition to become "an honest man, and labor truly."

Laboring "truly" for a living was not always easy. Many Londoners worked as domestic servants, and their prospects depended to a great extent on the whims of their employers. Servants could be fired for various causes, including charges of immoral behavior, and the nature of domestic service could easily lead to such accusations. The majority of English youths between the ages of 15 and 24 worked as servants, and at a time of life when

sexual desire ran high, they were thrown together in close quarters. Only a small percentage could afford to marry, leaving them with few options other than celibacy or illicit affairs. A lack of chastity could mean dismissal and, for women, confinement to a place like Bridewell for rehabilitation.

Those who became the object of their employers' desires were in a tight spot whether they yielded or refused. Men as well as women—and other live-in employees as well as domestics—had to walk a fine line between pleasing their amorous masters or mistresses and protecting their own reputations. The romantic perils of household service were well documented by a handsome and gifted music tutor named Thomas Whythorne, who had to cater to the fancies of the wealthy for many years before achieving success on his own.

In another era, Thomas Whythorne might have avoided the pitfalls of domestic employment altogether. Although his father, a landowner in Somersetshire, had not been able to provide adequately for all his children, young Thomas had been placed with

Goodwives' Recipes for Feasting and Fly Catching

After breakfasting on cereal or bacon, the mistress of a household, or goodwife, turned her thoughts to the midday dinner, her family's main repast. If guests were coming or if winter had reduced the supply of fresh food, she might consult a manuscript or a printed "receipt book" for recipes. A capable goodwife needed no advice on roasting a chicken or a joint of

beef, but a recipe could be necessary when making a complicated filling for a main-dish pie or a pungent sauce to mask the taste of old mutton.

Receipt books also helped with two of the matron's biggest challenges: preserving meats and varying the dishes eaten on the 153 annual "fish days." Potting veal in a thick layer of butter or sousing pork in vinegar and bay leaves proved appetizing alternatives to the common practice of salting meats to preserve them. And eel pie, stewed oysters, and broiled mackerel

with gooseberry garnish were welcome respites from boiled fish.

In the well-to-do household, fresh vegetables were artfully cooked or arranged in fancy "sallets," or salads, while fresh fruit—which was no longer thought to be unhealthy as in medieval days—was served in the preferred forms of puddings, tarts, and trifles. A favorite ingredient to be found in dessert recipes was dried fruit; in fact, one foreign ambassador claimed that the English were known to hang themselves if they could not afford to pur-

Glassware, loaves of bread called manchet, wine, and a large fowl mark the host of this meal as a man of means. Place settings rarely included forks, which had been introduced from Italy and were regarded as an effeminate novelty.

TO MAKE A MARROW~BONE PIE

To bake the best marrow~bone pie, after you have mixt the crusts of the best sort of pastes, and raised the coffin in such manner as you please; you shall first in the bottome thereof lay a course of marrowe of a Beefe mixt with Currants, then upon it a lay of the soales of Artichocks after they have been boiled and are divided from the thistle, then cover them over with marrow, currants, and great Raysons the stones pickt out; then lay a course of Potatos cut in thicke slices after they have beene boiled soft and are cleane pild; then cover them with marrow, currants, great raysons, suger and cinamon; Then lay a layer of candied Erringo roots mixt very thicke with the slices of Dates: Then cover it with marrow, currants, great reasins, suger, cinamon and dates, with a few damaske prunes, and so bake it; And after it is bakt power into it as long as it will receive it white wine, rosewater, suger, cinamon, and vinegar, mixt together, and candy all the cover with rosewater, and suger onely: And so set it into the oven a little, and after serve it foorth.

A pie recipe calls for candied eryngo root—the root of the evergreen herb sea holly—and a brand-new addition to the English larder from the New World: sweet potatoes. The coffin is a pastry shell.

TO MAKE A FOOLE

Take the top of the mornings milk, boile it with some whole mace & nutmeg cut in quarters, when you take it from the fire put in a piece of butter into it, then have manchet cut thin, & poure the Creame hot upon it; so let it stand till it bee almost cold, then put to it the whites of two eggs, & the yolks of five & some sugar & rosewater, & two spoonfulls of seck, & a little salt, mingle it altogether & straine it, & put some currance into it, put it in a dish & bake it, & so serve it. You must make the stuf no thicker than batter.

Elizabethans loved sugar, using it not only in desserts like fool *(above)*, but also in wine, omelets, and icings for meat pies.

DIVERS EXCELLENT KINDES OF BOTTLE ALE TO BE MADE WITH THE AFORESAID OYLES

I Cannot remember that ever I did drinke the like sage ale at any time, as that which is made by mingling two or three droppes of good oyle of sage, with a quart of Ale . . . And this waie a whole stande of sage Ale is speedily made. The like is to be done with the oyle of mace, or nutmegs . . . Some commend the hanging of a rosted Orenge prickt full of Cloves, in the vessell of Ale, till you find the tast thereof sufficiently mended to your owne liking.

Children and adults alike commonly drank ale or beer with their meals, including breakfast. Water was generally avoided unless it was distilled with roses or herbs.

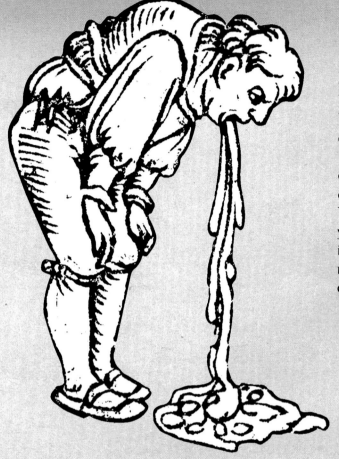

chase currants for their holiday dishes.

Printed receipt books were not for the poor. Even if they could read, they could not afford the books or the exotic ingredients that many of the recipes required. The lower class subsisted mainly on brown bread and so-called white meats—eggs and dairy products.

The same receipt book that provided culinary inspiration served as a handbook of home remedies and household hints. The goodwife did not need to look beyond her garden for many of the requisite ingredients. She boiled, distilled, and dried roses and violets to make medicinal powders, syrups, and lozenges, as well as pleasant "hand waters" to wash up with before and after meals. She made herb "simples" in lieu of visiting the apothecary. Dew, earthworms, and snails figured in her arsenal of remedies. May dew and fluid from pricked snails were said to soothe sore eyes; earthworms boiled in oil and wine supposedly eased aching joints.

After a busy day of brewing, cleaning, conserving, cooking, distilling, and doctoring, the goodwife might treat herself to a well-deserved warm caudle of spiced ale and milk thickened with breadcrumbs and egg yolks. She might then sprinkle rosemary leaves under her bed to ensure sweet dreams.

Medicinal recipes included antidotes for drunkenness *(below)* and for venery, or sexual desire, for the unmarried *(right)*. Elizabethan authorities became increasingly concerned about public inebriation and the spread of a new venereal disease, syphilis.

ANTIDOTES TO VENERY

If thy loins be too hot, anoint them with the oil of henbane or poppy . . . and do not . . . lie in a soft featherbed. Some there be which cool their privities in cold water, and find thereby a present remedy. They that drink the juice of water lily . . . 12 days together shall have no manner of desire to carnality. And therefore it is good for wiveless bachelors and husbandless maidens to drink.

HOW TO MAKE DRUNKARDS LOATHE WINE

To make common drunkards loathe and abhor wine, put a live eel in a wide~mouthed pot of wine deep enough to suffocate it. Give the strained wine to the drunkard to drink.

Many receipt books offered advice on getting rid of vermin and insects (right), attracted by refuse tossed just outside a city dweller's door. Of course, some women simply attacked such uninvited houseguests with a broom.

HOW TO KEEPE FLYES FROM OILE PEECES

Pricke a Cowcumber full of barley cornes with the small spiring ends outward, make little holes in the Cowcumber first with a woodden or bone bodkin, and after put in the graine, these beeing thicke placed will in time cover all the Cowcumber, so as no man can discerne what strange plant the same should bee. Such Cowcumbers are to bee hung up in the middest of summer roomes to drawe all the flies unto them, which otherwise would flie upon the pictures or hangings.

a generous uncle near Oxford. After discerning that the boy had a musical gift, the uncle sent him off to study music at Oxford. But any hopes the uncle had of young Whythorne's gaining a prestigious post as a church musician were set back by England's ongoing reformation, which began when Whythorne was a boy. Congregational singing began to replace the organ and choir in many Protestant churches, and the opportunities for church musicians diminished. Instead, Whythorne would spend much of his career as a music tutor.

In his early twenties, Whythorne entered a great house in London to assume the first of many posts he would hold over the next two decades as a tutor. Although he probably longed in his heart for something better, he was outwardly genial, and by his own account, many of the women around him found him attractive. One day a servant girl slipped romantic verses into the strings of his gittern, a kind of guitar Whythorne often played. He wrote a gently discouraging response in verse to his correspondent, hoping to end the matter discreetly. But as Whythorne later recorded in his memoirs, the event soon became "known all about the house . . . which made me to blush, and she more so." The girl soon suffered more than just embarrassment, however. When the master and mistress heard the tale, they dismissed her.

Whythorne tried to avoid such unfortunate incidents in the future by maintaining a friendly but distant relationship with the women he worked with and for. As he put it, he could "be merry with them," but he had no business making love to them "by word, sign or deed, especially in deed." But that tactic was of little use when the mistress of the house insisted on more. At one point, Whythorne reluctantly accepted a position as both tutor and servant to a wealthy widow. He compared a servant's lot to that of a water spaniel, commanded to "fetch or bring here, or carry there with all kind of drudgery." But the chief burden of his new position proved to be of a subtler nature. His mistress loved to have men pining after her and bragged about how she could "with a frown make them look pale and how with a merry look she could make them to joy again." He soon became the object of her flirtation. Realizing he had little choice but to play along if he wanted to keep his job, he decided to make the most of it.

Noticing that she seemed jealous when other women paid attention to him, he wrote her love verses, expressing his devotion in suitably ambiguous terms, lest she think him too forward. It seemed to do the trick. She took a lively interest in his appearance, advising him at one point on what sort of rings and clothes to wear. Whythorne replied coyly that he would gladly wear such things for her sake if only he had the money to purchase them. He soon received from his obliging mistress cash and costly fabric to be made into new apparel. And so, he wrote, he obtained many precious items he might "peradventure have gone without."

Whythorne played a game fraught with hazards. To please his lady, he was not simply "pleasant and merry" but also "somewhat bold with her." Not bold enough, apparently, for she scoffed that he "lacked audacity." But the tutor could not afford to go too far. Their flirtation was already "much talked of in the house," he noted, and anything truly scandalous might destroy his reputation and leave him without a future. While admitting that Cupid's "fiery arrows . . . did heat us a little," he insisted that they remained chaste. Eventually, they were delivered from temptation when his mistress lost a significant part of her fortune and had

Amateur singers and musicians, like the couple playing stringed instruments at left, avidly sought the latest madrigals, consort songs, and lute airs from London publishers. Some Elizabethans hired gifted tutors such as composer Thomas Whythorne (below) to teach them to read music, a skill considered a mark of gentility.

to release him from her employ. Though Whythorne feathered his nest a bit in the service of his amorous employer, his career as a music tutor did not bring him much wealth. He was something of an ornament in the great houses he worked in, much like the musical instruments themselves, which well-to-do Elizabethans used to decorate their homes even if they lacked musical talent. With the help of tutors such as Whythorne, however, many tried to learn at least one instrument, such as the lute—favored as an accompaniment to song, for which Elizabethans had a genuine passion.

Many also sought instruction in the singing of madrigals, a musical form performed by several voices that Whythorne helped to popularize in England. He made a name for himself by composing some of his own and publishing the first book of English madrigals, in 1571. Shortly afterward, he achieved the sort of distinction he had often longed for when he was appointed master of music for Matthew Parker, archbishop of Canterbury, who shared Queen Elizabeth's fondness for sacred music and helped preserve choirs and organs as part of the Church of England. For all Whythorne's romantic misadventures as a young man, he finally settled down to married life when he was nearly 50. He retained to his dying day a profound devotion to music, which he considered a divine gift, granted by God "unto His angels and ministers before the world began."

While some resourceful Elizabethans were making careers in music, others were playing to the public's growing enthusiasm for drama. Not long after Whythorne published his collection of madrigals, the first permanent playhouse, named simply the Theatre, opened in a London suburb. Spurred by its success, competing playhouses soon appeared, each with its own acting company. Unlike strolling players moving from town to town, London-based troupes vying for audiences in the city constantly sought new plays to add to their repertoire to lure customers and keep them coming. Among those who filled that need were some brilliant playwrights who perfected their command of the language and honed their dramatic skills not at the university but on the stage itself. One such theatrical prodigy was Ben Jonson, a one-time bricklayer whose accomplishments rivaled those of William Shakespeare, another playwright of modest education and towering talent. Jonson's own life was a drama, filled with harrowing predicaments and narrow escapes.

Ben Jonson never knew his father, who died a

and reckless, he challenged an enemy soldier to single combat in between the two encampments. Jonson killed his opponent and relieved the corpse of its costly armor and weapons.

After returning home, Jonson married and set out to make a living in London as an actor and playwright. His stint in the army served him well, for Elizabethan actors waged wars both on and off the stage. Companies vied for supremacy, and rivals traded blows in taverns and back alleys. In addition, performers whose work angered the government could be arrested and their plays shut down. In 1597 Jonson performed in a controversial play that he had helped complete for the stage after another dramatist left it unfinished. Entitled *The Isle of Dogs,* it incensed members of the queen's Privy

> *"Have mercy upon me,*
> *O God, according to thy loving kindness:*
> *According unto the multitude of thy tender mercies*
> *blot out my transgressions."*

short time before Jonson was born in 1572. His mother later married a bricklayer from Charing Cross. The boy himself also seemed to be destined for a life of mortar and bricks, until a family friend secured him a place at Westminster School, a prestigious academy associated with Westminster Abbey and patronized by the queen. Though Jonson proved an able student, steeping himself in classical literature, he failed to secure a scholarship to continue his studies and had to leave school around the age of 16. For a time he took up his stepfather's trade but sought escape from the tedium in the early 1590s by joining the army in a campaign against Spanish forces in the Netherlands. Bold

Council, who promptly had Jonson and two others involved in the production arrested and confined at the Marshalsea Prison in Southwark.

Some members of the troupe managed to avoid imprisonment by fleeing town, and Jonson did what he could to protect them, refusing under interrogation to reveal where the other players could be found and who had participated in writing the play or had copies of it. The Privy Council was intent on destroying every copy of the play and succeeded to the extent that it was lost to posterity. Jonson would later brag that his inquisitors "could get nothing of him to all their demands but 'Aye' and

'No.'" Frustrated, they placed "two damned villains" in his cell to lure him into some disclosure. But the playwright had made a friend of the jail keeper, who alerted him to this ploy, and Jonson revealed nothing. Finally, the authorities released Jonson and his co-horts—after issuing a warning to the entire theater profession by closing down London's playhouses for several months.

But the fiery playwright would soon be behind bars once again. In the fall of 1598, as he was beginning to enjoy his first notable success for his comedy *Every Man in His Humour,* he was ar-rested for killing an actor named Gabriel Spencer with a weapon described in the indictment as a "sword of iron and steel called a rapier, of the price of three shillings." Jon-son claimed that Spencer had forced the duel, but a jury listening to the facts indicted him on a charge of manslaughter. Evidently believing a trial would turn out no better, Jonson pleaded guilty to the charge and tried to save himself by claim-ing "benefit of clergy."

This archaic loophole in English law had been instituted in the 13th century at the insistence of the medieval church, which sought to protect priests and others who worked for the church from prosecution in secular courts. Defendants who could prove themselves to be clergy had to be handed over to the church for trial, except in certain cases such as rape. At first, the test had been rigorous, but it had eventually been reduced to one basic

Drama critics sometimes attacked playwright Ben Jonson *(left)* personally. One derided the former bricklayer as a "brown-bread mouth stinker," brown bread being a lower-class staple. Another compared his graceless gait to that of a bear.

skill: the ability to read a pas-sage from the Bible in Latin. That made sense in the Mid-dle Ages, when literacy had been largely confined to the clergy, but by the 16th cen-tury, many men with no con-nection to the church could qualify. Women, however, could not claim the benefit because they were barred from the clergy. They could "plead their bellies," or claim to be pregnant, but that was at most a nine-month stay of execution.

Those pleading benefit of clergy were often asked to read the first verse of the 51st Psalm, fre-quently called the "neck verse" because it saved so many con-victed men from hanging. "Have mercy upon me, O God," its English translation began, "according to thy loving kindness: / According unto the multitude of thy tender mercies blot out my transgressions." This was no great challenge for the highly liter-ate Jonson, who thus escaped hanging. (Some illiterate prisoners gained their freedom by committing the verse to memory.) Nor did the playwright face a church trial since the Protestant estab-lishment no longer required that the thousands of criminals claiming the benefit be subjected to even a perfunctory trial. Yet Jonson did not avoid punishment altogether. As mandated in such

Booksellers and Bestsellers

Londoners in search of a good read headed for the churchyard of St. Paul's Cathedral, where an army of booksellers and printers had set up shop. They did an ever-expanding business there as a result of the wider use of the printing press, the spread of literacy, and the printing of books in English as well as Latin (once the only accepted language for serious writing). The demand for retail space at St. Paul's was so great that the underground vault of a burial chapel was cleared of its bones and two privies at either end of the cathedral were built over—much to the inconvenience and discomfort of local residents and pupils at St. Paul's school.

To attract customers, booksellers pasted their walls and stallboards with effusively worded title pages from recent publications and stationed apprentices outside to get the attention of passersby. Patrons who entered the Blazing Star, the Three Pigeons, and other nearby shops found items to suit all budgets and tastes. A laborer might choose a popular ballad such as "When Jesus Christ was 12," while the discriminating courtier or lady might purchase Sir Philip Sidney's pastoral romance *The Arcadia.* Much of the space on booksellers' shelves was taken up with Bibles, grammars, and almanacs, the last offering advice on when to plant, administer medicine, and engage

Two pressmen cover pages of type with ink and prepare the paper for printing, while behind them a pair of compositors consult manuscripts and set type. A London press could turn out 250 sheets an hour.

Workers dig for human bones at Stonehenge in this engraving from *Britannia (above)*, a best-selling book on English history and antiquities. It was written by Ben Jonson's schoolmaster William Camden.

John Foxe's vividly illustrated story of martyrs *(left)* was one of the most influential books of the age. Despite its steep price, it went through five editions and sold more than 10,000 copies during Elizabeth's reign.

in sex. Domestic conduct books, also widely read, dealt with such topics as wife beating and arranged marriages.

Drama enthusiasts might find cheap copies of favorite plays, though these were often unauthorized versions based on actors' memories or notes scribbled during performances rather than the original manuscripts. A line such as "To be or not to be, that is the question," from Shakespeare's *Hamlet,* for example, became "To be or not to be, ay, there's the point" in such works.

One of England's busiest readers was the bishop of London, who as of 1586 shared with the archbishop of Canterbury and their assistants the task of licensing books to ensure political and religious orthodoxy. With more than 3,000 new titles issued in the last decade of Elizabeth's reign by approved printing houses, bootleggers, and secret Catholic presses, the bishop lamented that "these printers will be the death of me."

THE Bloudy booke, OR, The Tragicall and desperate end of Sir *John Fites* (alias) *Fitz.*

The Apprehension and confession of three notorious Witches. **Arreigned and by Iustice condemned and** executed at *Chelmes-forde,* in the Countye of *Essex, the 5. day of Iulye, last past.* 1589. ¶ With the manner of their diuelish practices and keeping of their spirits, whose fourmes are heerein truelye proportioned.

IOAN PRENTIS & hir Bid

IACKE

GILL

In the news pamphlet above, subtitled "The Tragicall and Desperate End of Sir John Fites," a madman kills himself after attacking an innocent couple. In a second pamphlet *(left),* a ferret-shaped spirit attends a witch, who is later hanged with two other women. Crimes, monstrous births, and freak storms filled the pages of cheap popular publications; other domestic news, such as politics, was strictly controlled by the government.

Itinerant peddlers hawked pamphlets, ballads, and chapbooks at fairs and markets. Officials suspected—often rightly—that they carried papist or seditious works in their packs.

Townsmen fight a losing battle against fire with buckets and hooks. Stories of such conflagrations were read with horrified interest by the many Elizabethans living in timber-and-thatch houses.

Newes from all parties is in my sacke

with lies and tales it Loades my backe

To the f ...nde ...an

cases, authorities confiscated his property and branded him on the base of his left thumb—a sign that he had claimed benefit of clergy once and could never do so again.

That Jonson qualified as a clergyman under a Protestant government was ironic, for he had converted to Catholicism while in prison and distanced himself from the Church of England. In 1606 a church court called him to account for failing to take Communion as the law required. Jonson confessed that he had refused Communion as a matter of conscience. Once again, he found his way out of a legal bind, this time by promising to confer with learned Protestants and consider their arguments. And in fact, several years later, he returned to the Protestant fold.

All the while, Jonson's reputation as a writer was growing, thanks in part to the same instrument that advanced the career of Thomas Whythorne—the printing press. Jonson was not the first playwright to have his work set in print. Some of the plays of Shakespeare and others had been published, but they were unauthorized versions filled with mistakes or scripts sold by the acting companies to the printer, who then held the copyright. Beginning in 1600, Jonson published his own work, "as it was first composed," according to the title page, meaning without alterations for the stage. In doing so, he sought to be judged as a man of letters rather than as a mere playwright. He attracted the support of Sir Robert Townsend and other wealthy patrons of gifted writers. Ultimately, Jonson acquired protégés of his own, rising young writers who referred to themselves as the "sons of Ben" and who looked to the master for inspiration. The former bricklayer had become one of the city's literary monuments.

Among those who followed the exploits of Ben Jonson, William Shakespeare, and other luminaries of London with keen interest was a law student named John Manningham, who kept a diary that revealed much about the city and its leading personalities. Hobnobbing with the famous was one of the privileges of students at the Inns of Court, the four elite law academies in London. In the words of Ben Jonson, the Inns were the "noblest nurseries of humanity and liberty in the kingdom." Manningham studied at perhaps the finest of the four, the Middle Temple, and shared the broad interests and enthusiasms of others who pursued law, the all-purpose field of study for gentlemen of the day. They trained at a leisurely pace, and Manningham had plenty of time to dine and converse with the city's notables and record in his diary their jests, gibes, and retorts.

ENGLAND'S BARD

Son of an illiterate glover, William Shakespeare left school at a young age. But a voracious appetite for reading and a natural ear for language more than compensated for his abbreviated education and allowed him to become England's greatest playwright.

Born in 1564, Shakespeare moved to London around age 23 and began performing and writing for Lord Chamberlain's Men, a prominent acting troupe. During the 1590s, his career flourished as he penned a score of historical dramas, comedies, and tragedies, such as *Richard III, A Midsummer Night's Dream,* and *Romeo and Juliet.* In 1599 the Bard, as he would come to be known, became the principal playwright of the Globe Theatre, and in the next few years produced his greatest tragedies: *Hamlet, Othello, Macbeth,* and *King Lear.*

After Elizabeth's death in 1603, Shakespeare became a member of the prestigious acting troupe the King's Men, under the patronage of her successor, James I. Shrewd theater investments allowed the Bard to retire to his hometown of Stratford-upon-Avon in 1613, where he died three years later. Members of the King's Men published the first collected edition of his works in 1623 *(right).* Despite efforts to discredit Shakespeare's authorship in recent times, most scholars firmly believe these great plays were written by the glover's son from Stratford.

MR. WILLIAM
SHAKESPEARES
COMEDIES,
HISTORIES, &
TRAGEDIES.

Published according to the True Originall Copies.

LONDON
Printed by Iſaac Iaggard, and Ed. Blount. 1623.

In 1602 he set down a tale about Shakespeare that had been making the rounds. A celebrated actor named Richard Burbage was playing the title role in Shakespeare's *Richard III,* a stirring account of the ruthless king who fell in battle to Henry Tudor, Elizabeth's grandfather, thus launching the Tudor dynasty. A woman watching Burbage perform reportedly was so taken by him that she invited him to visit her after the show, instructing him to announce himself as Richard III. Shakespeare overheard her invitation and decided that he would take advantage of the situation. The playwright reached her lair ahead of the actor, related Manningham, and "was entertained, and at his game ere Burbage came." While Shakespeare was still there, Richard III was announced. Shakespeare, invoking historical precedent, informed the belated Burbage that "William the Conqueror was before Richard III."

A similar spirit of playful competition prevailed between Manningham and his comrades at the Middle Temple. The students staged their own dramas and revels on festive occasions in the Middle Temple's handsome new hall near the Thames. On All Saints' Day (November 1) and Candlemas (February 2), for example, the Inn entertained distinguished alumni with a lavish banquet, which was often accompanied by a performance. At times the playfulness degenerated into rowdiness, however, and students were fined for such misdeeds as gambling with dice and making "outcries in the night." A particular source of aggravation to those in the vicinity of the Inn, where the students lived two to a chamber, was their nasty habit of tossing the contents of chamber pots "and other annoyances" out the window, "to the great offence of gentlemen of good worth passing by," as an ordinance of the Middle Temple put it. That misdemeanor warranted a fine of 40 shillings.

There was a good deal more to Manningham's education in London than high jinks and carousing. Son of a gentleman with secure roots in the landed gentry, he had been adopted after his father's death by a relative who owned an estate in Kent and kept the privileged young man on a safe course that led to Cambridge University and on to the Middle Temple. Unlike many other comfortable sons of the gentry at the Inns of Court, who went there largely to socialize and never practiced law, however, Manningham was determined to make something of the opportunity and enhance his fortune. Some of his fellow students applied themselves for a different reason. They came from families of sufficient means but little distinction and saw the profession as their route to respectability. As one Elizabethan writer pointed out, "Whosoever studieth the laws of the realm . . . shall be taken for a gentleman."

To qualify as a barrister, or a lawyer who could plead in court, Manningham first spent seven years studying at the Middle Temple. There he participated in hypothetical law cases called moots, read law as well as history and literature, and attended so-called Grand Readings conducted by senior lawyers that took place twice a year and lasted three to four weeks. In due course, Manningham took the Oath of Supremacy to become an Utter Barrister, but he was required to continue mooting for two more years before being allowed to practice law. And even then he would remain under the discipline of the Inns of Court for the remainder of his career.

Manningham was now an actor in his chosen theater—a legal arena that was growing busier by the year as cases concerning debt, land disputes, contracts, and slander proliferated. "The first thing we do, let's kill all the lawyers," proposed one of Shakespeare's characters. But it was the public and its litigious nature that kept the lawyers busy. Manningham was appointed to the Court of Wards and Liveries, which oversaw wards of the Crown, including widows and minor heirs of deceased landowners and mentally incompetent property holders. The officials of the court raised money for the Crown—and profited themselves—by leasing out the lands of those wards and by selling wardships to people who agreed to take responsibility for children under the court's supervision. Predictably, this system generated lawsuits, and suitors had no choice but to employ Manningham and his colleagues. One Elizabethan poet bemoaned the fate of a man who initiated a suit in the Court of Wards and kept at it fruitlessly for seven years: "Ah wretched man, in mothers womb accurst, / That could'st not rather lose thy suit at first."

Manningham married into the firm, as it were, by wedding the daughter of William Curle, one of the court's two auditors. The successful young lawyer divided his days between his legal duties in and around London and his family responsibilities in the country. Not long after their marriage, the Manninghams and their two small children took up residence in Kent to help John's adoptive father manage his estate there, which Manningham inherited when the old man died. In London, meanwhile, he maintained chambers at the Middle Temple, his second home, where his connections to other members of that select legal fraternity continued to bring him satisfaction and profit.

Despite the proud English tradition of allowing defendants jury trials, the accused in Elizabethan times enjoyed few of the legal protections that would be taken for granted in later days. Defendants accused of felonies, for example, stood alone to answer the charges against them at trial unless a point of law arose that required counsel. The burden of proof fell on the prosecution, and the accused could challenge jurors considered hostile. But suspects imprisoned in the infamous Tower of London on charges of treason might languish in confinement for years without

Law student John Manningham and his fellows gathered in Middle Temple Hall *(right)* for legal readings and practice cases known as moots as well as for meals, revels, and plays, including a staging of Shakespeare's *Twelfth Night,* performed by the Bard's own company. Stylish apparel, such as courtiers' boots and cloaks, was banned; students wore sober-colored scholars' gowns.

receiving a trial. And they could be subjected to torture by officials who had various ways of forcing prisoners to betray their confederates or confess to deeds that they might or might not have committed.

In April 1597 a Jesuit priest named John Gerard was summoned from his cell in the forbidding structure known to Londoners simply as the Tower to face questioning. Built originally as a fortress in the 11th century, the Tower had been expanded over the centuries and now covered some 18 acres along the north bank of the Thames, east of London Bridge. It included a central bastion, 90 feet high, known as the White Tower, ringed by inner and outer walls incorporating several smaller towers, beyond which lay a watery moat 100 feet across, flanked by a third and final wall. Few inmates had ever escaped from the Tower, but Gerard, after suffering torment there, would make a daring attempt at freedom.

After being led from his cell under guard, Gerard found himself before a formidable group of royal officials, including Francis Bacon, a man of keen intellect who had

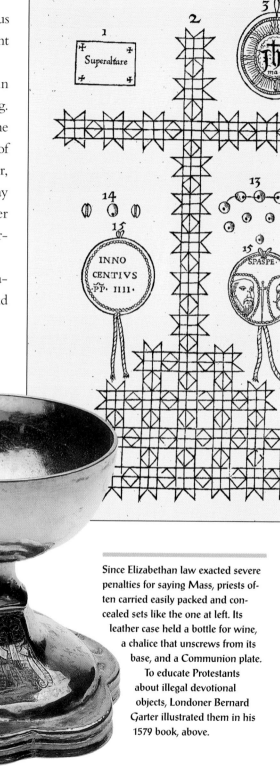

Since Elizabethan law exacted severe penalties for saying Mass, priests often carried easily packed and concealed sets like the one at left. Its leather case held a bottle for wine, a chalice that unscrews from its base, and a Communion plate. To educate Protestants about illegal devotional objects, Londoner Bernard Garter illustrated them in his 1579 book, above.

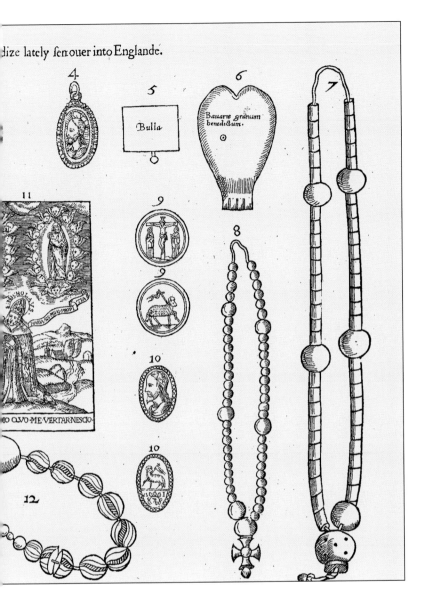

dize lately fent ouer into Englande.

4
5
Bulla
6
Bauariæ granum benedictum.
7
11
9
9
8
10
10
12

What about the letters he had recently received from abroad, one of his inquisitors wanted to know. Now Gerard knew why he had been brought to the Tower. While tending furtively to the needs of Catholics in England, he had corresponded with his fellow Jesuits. Even in the Clink, he had received letters from abroad, which he had read and then smuggled out of prison to Father Henry Garnet, the Jesuit superior in England, who had thus far eluded arrest. Evidently an informer had learned of those letters—though he had not seen their actual contents—and had alerted authorities.

Though serving as a Catholic priest was now a treasonous act in England, Gerard's questioners evidently hoped to force the priest to admit that he sought to overthrow not just Protestantism but Elizabeth herself. And they hoped that he would implicate others. But Gerard refused to reveal the name of the man who acted as his courier.

"We'll see to it that you tell us," said one of his inquisitors, who handed Gerard a warrant from the Privy Council authorizing his torture—a warrant easily obtained at a time when missionary priests were routinely regarded as enemy agents.

In a sense, Gerard had been preparing all his life for this moment. Born to a Catholic family in 1564, he had seen his father imprisoned for three years for participating in a failed plot in 1570 to rescue Mary, Queen of Scots. Later, as a young man, Gerard fled the country in order to pursue his Jesuit education. Then in 1588, three years after Parliament passed a law expelling all Catholic priests from the country, his superiors sent the newly ordained Gerard, at his own request, home to England. He could not have chosen a more dangerous time for his return. Anti-Catholic sentiment was reaching new heights as a result of the attempted invasion of England by Spain's Catholic forces, led by the celebrated Armada. "The Spanish Fleet had exasperated the people against the Catholics," Gerard later wrote, "everywhere a hunt was being organized for Catholics and their houses

studied law in London at Gray's Inn and would become Lord Chancellor under Elizabeth's successor, James I. Bacon and his fellow inquisitors wanted to know about the priest's political activities. Gerard, who had recently been transferred to the Tower after spending three years in a London prison called the Clink, reminded them that he had been "examined time and time again, and they had not produced a scrap of writing or a single trustworthy witness to show that I had taken part in any activities against the government."

searched." Yet Gerard forged ahead with missionary zeal, crossing from France in November.

The boat left the young priest at a deserted spot along the Norfolk coast, where Catholic sentiment remained strong and Gerard had a decent chance of finding refuge. After huddling in the woods through the cold rainy night, he strolled calmly out into the open, pretending to be a falconer searching for a stray hawk and wandering the countryside until he came across an admitted Catholic who agreed to shelter him. Over the next six years, several Catholic gentry harbored him in their homes, and as he traveled from place to place in disguise, he encouraged people to preserve their old faith—or to return to the fold. Even after he was captured and imprisoned in the Clink in 1594, he found kindred souls there and drew comfort from the correspondence that he received from abroad. But now, after being transferred to the Tower, he had to face the ultimate test of his faith: torture at the hands of authorities who wanted him to renounce his principles and betray his superior.

He underwent that trial in a dungeon in the White Tower, where attendants led him to one of the wooden pillars supporting the roof. Clasping his wrists in iron, they left him dangling from the pillar at such a height that his feet could barely touch the ground—then dug away the earth from beneath his toes. It was a slow torture, bloodless but excruciating, designed to break his spirit and wrest from him the name of the courier and the whereabouts of his Jesuit superior. Whenever Gerard fainted, the guards would place a set of wicker steps under his feet until he regained consciousness, only to renew the ordeal when they heard him begin to pray. At the end of the day, Gerard was taken down from the pillar and returned to his cell. The next morning, when he again refused to divulge his secret, the torture began afresh. Later, in his agony, he prayed aloud for the

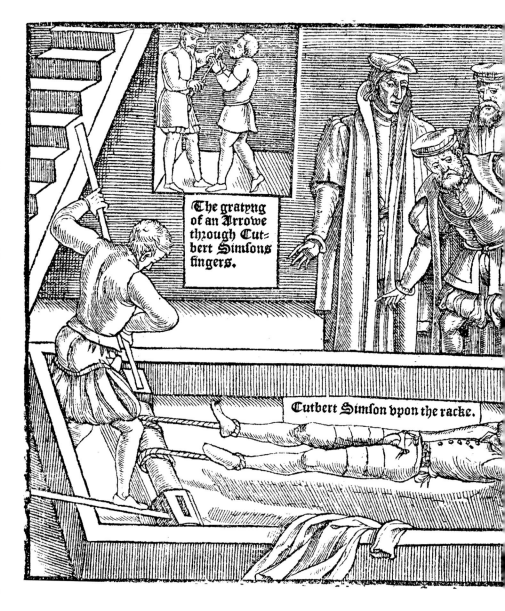

The gratyng of an Arrowe through Cutbert Simsons fingers.

Cutbert Simson vpon the racke.

As interrogators watch, a prisoner in the Tower of London is tortured on the rack, his joints stretched and dislocated. Other methods of torture are used on the same man in the background: An arrow is stabbed through his fingers *(top left)*, and a device called Skeffington's gyves, or irons *(shown at far right)*, compresses his body into a broken ball *(top right)*.

The scription howe Cutbert Simson stoode in an engine of Jron three houres, within the Tower, commonly called Scevington's gives.

strength to be "rent in pieces" before he should betray anyone. Impressed by his resolve, the examiners decided that there was little to gain from further torture.

Gerard had withstood the test, but he remained in peril. Others in his position had been tried, convicted, and sentenced to death after undergoing torture. Gerard found some solace, however, in the person of his warder, a man called Bennett who had carried him gently back to his cell from the torture chamber. Now Bennett became his nurse.

Such a close relationship between warder and prisoner was not surprising in Elizabethan prisons, where prison officials frequently relied on prisoners to supplement their meager wages. These payments largely accounted for the vast differences in living conditions between the common prisoner and the inmate of means. Those who could pay their jailers well enjoyed good food and drink and were even allowed to practice a trade in prison. They could dine alone or with friends; in either event, they could be waited upon by their guards. But those who had nothing to offer had to fend for themselves as best they could. Gerard knew of one imprisoned gentlewoman who cooked and sewed for herself in order to save money to help poor Catholics in confinement.

Thus paid, Bennett cared for Gerard as he recovered from his injuries. So damaged were the priest's hands that he could not move his fingers, and the warder had to cut the prisoner's food into small pieces. Within three weeks, Gerard had regained the use of his fingers. Not long thereafter, he asked his warder to buy him some oranges and exercised his fingers by cutting the orange peels into small crosses, stitching the crosses together in pairs, and stringing them on a thread to create little rosaries. Covertly, he stored the orange juice in a jar.

Gerard told Bennett that he wished to send some rosaries to friends and requested paper to wrap them in. With the warder's permission, the priest then wrote a short note to his friends in charcoal. When Bennett was not watching, however, Gerard took a quill (which supposedly he had requested for picking his teeth), dipped it in the orange juice, and this time wrote another message, invisible to the naked eye, between the lines. Having used this clandestine method of communication before, he knew his friends would be looking for the hidden message. And indeed, upon receiving Gerard's note, they exposed the paper to heat, rendering the orange juice visible. They then wrote back to him by the same means, wrapping sweetmeats for Gerard in a seemingly blank piece of paper. Bennett willingly served as the courier for a fee. After months of this secret correspondence, the priest discovered that the subterfuge was unnecessary: Bennett was illiterate and could no more decipher the visible text than he could that which was hidden between the lines.

As yet, Gerard had not tried to enlist the help of his friends in an escape attempt from the Tower, but events would soon drive him to that desperate measure. Although he was officially allowed no visitors, two Catholic women managed to bribe their way into his cell while pretending to tour the Tower. They aroused no suspicion, because people often came to view the sights there—including the queen's own menagerie of lions and other exotic animals housed on the Tower's grounds. The two women gave Gerard alarming news. They had heard he would soon be subjected to a perfunctory trial that could have only one outcome: a sentence of death.

At first Gerard thought nothing of avoiding this fate but only of celebrating Mass before he died. He had none of the items he required for that purpose, but one of his fellow inmates—a Catholic by the name of John Arden, living under a sentence of death for having plotted 10 years earlier to free the late Queen Mary—was allowed visits from his wife. She might be able to

A bird's-eye view engraving shows the fortified complex known as the Tower of London as it appeared in 1597, the year of Jesuit priest John Gerard's incarceration there. The Salt Tower (M), where he was imprisoned, and the Cradle Tower (Q), where he started his perilous escape over the encircling moat to the wharf, are at lower right. An unsuccessful escape attempt by other prisoners resulted in the fatal aftermath shown below.

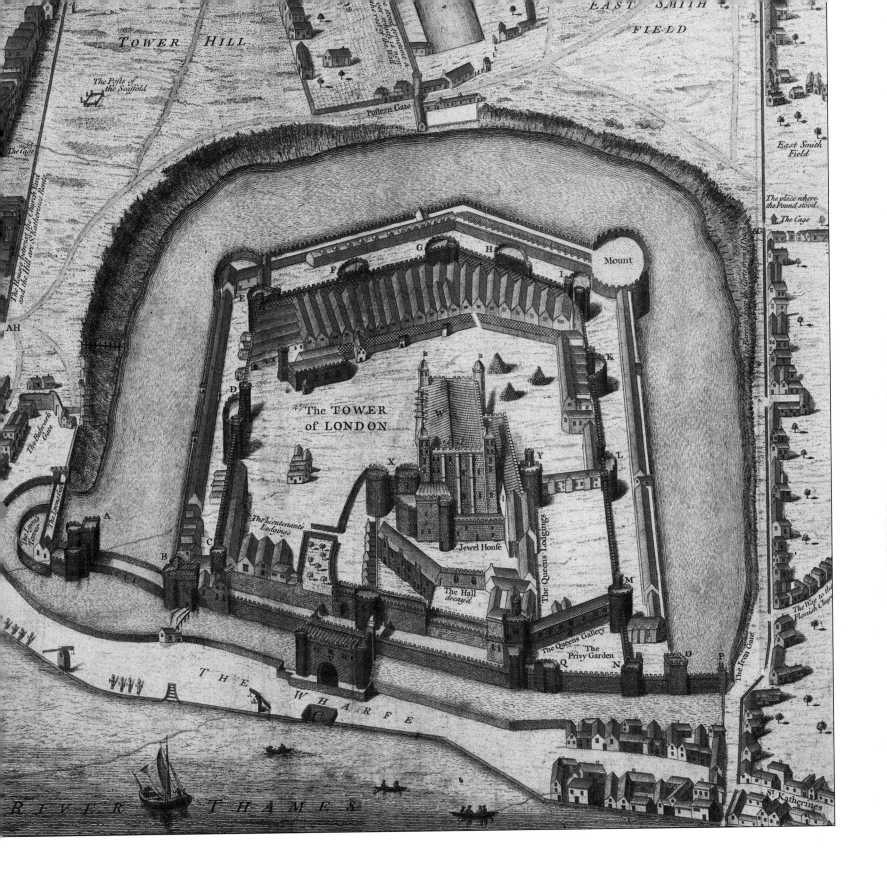

smuggle in what Gerard needed to say Mass for both men. Gerard bribed his warder to allow him to dine with Arden in the condemned man's cell, located in a tower in the outer wall. Once there, Gerard was struck by the proximity of the water-filled moat—and the Thames beyond. Perhaps the time had not yet come for him to celebrate his final Mass after all. Perhaps deliverance was within reach.

He and Arden worked out an escape plan, which required that they make their way in the night to the roof above Arden's cell and escape by means of a rope cast over the moat and the wall beyond it. Rescuers would then be awaiting them along the Thames. Gerard then dutifully wrote to Father Garnet for permission to attempt the escape, which he readily received, and sent letters to his friends recruiting their help. The first attempt was foiled when their rescuers

a thicker rope that they had secured to a stake. Gerard and Arden strained to haul the heavy rope back up to the tower, where they secured their end in preparation for the descent to freedom. They could see now how perilous it would be. The top of the wall beyond the moat was not much lower than the roof they were standing on, and the rope ran almost horizontally over the water. It would be a fearsome test of strength, and the least slip would land them in the moat.

After a brief moment of terror, Arden said, "I shall certainly be hanged if I remain here." He grasped the rope and made it safely across. Now it was Gerard's turn. But the rope had been slackened by the first man's descent, and Gerard was weak from his long imprisonment and torture. He had barely gone a few yards when his body swung around, and he nearly fell. He held on desperately, the black water licking

"I shall certainly be hanged if I remain here."

had to turn back after a chance encounter with a talkative stranger on the wharf outside the Tower. But they arranged to try again the next night.

Once more, Gerard bribed his way to Arden's cell. When the coast was clear, the two men forced the lock on the door in Arden's cell leading up to the roof and ascended the stairs, equipped with gear their friends had smuggled in to them for the attempt. The two men secured a long length of twine to the roof, and attached the other end to an iron ball. Spotting their accomplices, who had pinned white handkerchiefs to their clothes for identification, Gerard and Arden together heaved the heavy ball. The rescuers followed the sound of it hitting the ground to find the attached cord, which they untied and fastened to the free end of

the sides of the moat below. Moving slowly and with great effort, he finally reached the far side of the moat, but he lacked the strength to clear the wall. Seeing his plight, one of the rescuers scaled the wall and pulled Gerard to safety. Boarding their small boat, the men rowed away.

Although authorities searched for him, Gerard eluded their grasp. For almost a decade he remained in England as a priest. Then in 1606, he left the country disguised as a retainer to the Spanish ambassador and continued to work abroad for his order. Gerard's brilliant escape demonstrated a principle that many Londoners were embracing in this time of fierce trials and rich opportunities—a belief that the key to salvation, at least in this world, lay in one's own fortitude and ingenuity.

"All the World's a Stage"

"O! for a muse of fire, that would ascend / The brightest heaven of invention; / A kingdom for a stage, princes to act / And monarchs to behold the swelling scene." In the opening of William Shakespeare's *Henry V,* the chorus yearns for a grander theater and royal players to tell its story. But Elizabethans found London's playhouses and common-born actors thrilling enough for them, flocking daily to see plays such as *Henry V* and Thomas Kyd's drama of revenge, *The Spanish Tragedie (above).*

Playwrights such as Shakespeare, Kyd, Ben Jonson, and Christopher Marlowe transformed the medieval tradition of stilted morality plays into the vibrant and heady mix that was Elizabethan drama. With relevant plots, memorable characters, expressive imagery, and brilliant wordplay, the dramatic arts reached heights not attained since the golden age of Athens.

In the courtyard of a Coventry inn, guild members of the Shearmen and Taylors Company enact a miracle drama for a large crowd *(left)*. Above, an actor beats a troublesome heckler away from the stage, probably a typical occurrence among Elizabethan audiences, who often ate, drank, caroused, and brawled during a performance.

"The Play's the Thing"

Elizabethan drama had its beginnings in the medieval miracle plays, biblical stories acted out by monks within their cloisters and later by friars traveling the country to teach the faithful. By the Tudor era, local craft guilds were performing these dramas, as well as secular morality plays, for fellow townsmen on movable outdoor stages. Small troupes of traveling actors also provided entertainment on occasion, setting up at village fairs or in the courtyards of inns. But players often faced the wrath of town councilors, who feared the spread of plague and disliked the pickpockets and prostitutes attracted by the crowds.

The vagrancy act of 1572 classified all strolling players as vagabonds and barred them from performing without a license. Procuring a license required the patronage of wealthy nobles, which led to the formation of large London-based theater companies named for patrons. The Lord Chamberlain's Men, with Shakespeare as principal playwright, and Elizabeth's own troupe, the Queen's Players, were among the most prominent.

"People from all the corners of the land throng in heaps at thy fairs and thy theatres."

GLOBE . SOUTHWARKE

Theatergoers mingle outside the Globe *(left)*, which opened in 1599 with a performance of William Shakespeare's *Henry V.*

William Shakespeare *(right)* and other members of Lord Chamberlain's Men helped finance the Globe's construction, becoming "housekeepers," or shareholders, in the theater.

An actor sends an arrow soaring out of the Rose Theatre in this modern cutaway reconstruction depicting a performance of Shakespeare's *Titus Andronicus* in 1594. As indicated here, props and scenery were minimal, but great care was devoted to costuming, usually a theater company's greatest expense.

"The Great Globe Itself"

Keenly aware of the money to be made from London's drama fans, in 1574 actor James Burbage erected the first building specifically made for performing plays. Also the company manager of Leicester's Players, Burbage was familiar with city authorities' hostility toward the business and chose to build in the suburb of Shoreditch. Named simply The Theatre, it proved a success, and six more suburban playhouses—condemned by critics as wasteful foolishness—sprang up over the next 20 years. Five lay in seamy Southwark alongside the brothels and bearbaiting rings.

Many theaters were basically circular in shape and could hold 2,000 to 3,000 people. Thatched roofing provided protection for the three-tiered seating around the walls and at least partial covering for the stage, but the center pit was completely exposed. "Groundlings" paid a penny to stand in the pit, a rough area frequented by pickpockets and prostitutes. A sixpence bought a seat in the covered galleries, while the wealthiest patrons sat on the stage itself.

"Behold the sumptuous theatre-houses, a continual monument of London's prodigality and folly!"

Elizabethan theater produced both gifted tragedians and endearing clowns. James Burbage's son Richard, who performed the title roles in *Othello, Hamlet,* and *King Lear,* and Edward Alleyne, lead actor in Christopher Marlowe's plays, elicited an audience's deepest emotions, while Richard Tarlton and Will Kemp brought out its laughter.

Burbage and the others were greatly admired, and acting as a profession gained some respectability during their era. Yet it was still considered improper for women to act. Prepubescent boys, taught feminine gestures and voice, played the female roles. "[I] saw the tragedy of the first Emperor Julius with at least fifteen characters very well acted," wrote German visitor Thomas Platter, following a performance of Shakespeare's *Julius Caesar.* "At the end . . . they danced according to their custom with extreme elegance. Two in men's clothes and two in women's gave this performance."

"All the world's a stage, And all the men and women merely players. . . . And one man in his time plays many parts."

Faustus conjures up the devil in a scene from Marlowe's tale of a man who sells his soul *(above).* Edward Alleyne *(left)* played the doomed Faustus, as well as many other compelling roles, and a contemporary observed that he "so [acted] to the life that he made any part to become him."

The leading comic actor of his day, Richard Tarlton, shown at left with his trademark baggy pants and drum, was a favorite of Elizabeth's and a member of her troupe. According to dramatist Thomas Nashe, the actor was such a crowd pleaser that "people began exceedingly to laugh when Tarlton first peeped out his head."

In this scene from *Titus Andronicus,* Queen Tamora pleads for mercy for her son as a guard prepares to behead him. The only known contemporary illustration of a Shakespearean play, it shows the lead actors wearing the Roman costumes befitting the play's period.

115

Jones's costume designs were lavish and evocative: Sea-green skirts flow about the blue-tressed water spirit Oceania *(below),* while a fiery torchbearer is aflame in vivid red *(right).*

For the *Masque of Oberon*'s first scene, Inigo Jones designed a set containing an ominous-looking outcrop. Using an innovative technique involving painted shutters, the rocks opened to reveal a fairy palace.

A drawing by Jones illustrates his design for an elaborate two-sided stage mechanism that revolved on a pivot to reveal a costumed character. Lighting—presumably candles—covered the entire top of the set, giving a particularly dramatic effect.

"A Kingdom for a Stage"

A mix of poetry, music, and dance, the lavish performances called masques had been popular during Elizabeth's reign. But it was under her successor, James I, that the artistic collaboration of playwright Ben Jonson and renowned architect and designer Inigo Jones raised the production of the masques to its zenith. Jones, envisioning the performances as "Pictures with Light and Motion," created vibrant costumes and ingenious set designs to complement Jonson's colorful writing. Enormous amounts of time and money went into each performance, particularly those taking place in the ceremonial hall at Whitehall Palace during the annual Christmas festivities.

Both professional actors and the ladies and gentlemen of the court took part in the performances. The actors took on all the speaking parts, while the courtly masquers danced. To accommodate this division of the participants' roles, Jonson and Jones separated the masques into two dramatic parts. The first section portrayed the world in disorder and chaos and was performed by the actors. Then the dancers appeared in their fabulous costumes and restored the world to harmony.

117

SIC PARVIS MAGNA

1591

CHAPTER THREE

Dreams of Wealth and Glory

Sir Francis Drake stands proudly beside a globe evoking his celebrated voyage around the world, a feat for which he was knighted by Queen Elizabeth in 1581. A farmer's son, young Drake shipped out as a captain's apprentice and went on to become vice admiral of England, justifying the motto on his coat of arms: *Sic Parvis Magna,* or Greatness from Small Beginnings.

n April 1, 1581, Queen Elizabeth paid tribute to one of her most accomplished subjects, Francis Drake, who had returned six months earlier from a triumphant voyage around the world laden with treasure heisted from Spanish ships. His exploit had already earned him a hero's welcome at court and a handsome bonus from the queen, who allowed Drake to claim £10,000 of the plunder, which had a total worth of perhaps as much as £400,000. Now she was on her way to knight him aboard his vessel, the *Golden Hind,* in dry dock at Deptford, a few miles down the Thames from London. A boisterous crowd followed Elizabeth to the dock. So many well-wishers tried to board the ship after her that the plank collapsed under their weight and scores of people tumbled harmlessly into the mud below, scarcely dampening the festivities.

Drake hosted an extravagant banquet on the *Golden Hind* in the queen's honor and offered her further gifts, having already presented Elizabeth with a glittering prize from his booty—a crown studded with five emeralds, some as large as a little finger, the Spanish ambassador peevishly reported. In addition, she would claim a sizable share of the plunder as sovereign.

After the feasting, Drake knelt before Elizabeth to be knighted.

With a gilded sword in hand, she quipped that she would have Drake's head—a punishment that would no doubt please Spain's King Philip II, husband to her late sister, Mary Tudor. Then she handed the sword to a French envoy accompanying her and asked him to perform the honors. This was another jab at Philip, for the Frenchman was in England to try to negotiate a marriage between Elizabeth and his master, the duke of Anjou, in a strategic move against Spain. A short time earlier, amid the festivities, the French envoy had gallantly retrieved one of the queen's garters when it slipped from her leg and fell to the deck. Now he obliged her further by knighting Drake with the gilded sword.

When the captain of the *Golden Hind* arose, he was Sir Francis Drake—or as Elizabeth dubbed him, "our golden knight." His ship was placed on display at Deptford as a monument to England's new-found maritime power. But Sir Francis himself, the son of a farmer from Devonshire, was an even more impressive exhibit for a nation fast on the rise.

Drake's voyage and the royal hoopla attending his return deepened the enmity between Elizabeth and King Philip. He faulted her for aiding Dutch Protestant rebels against their Spanish Catholic overlords. She blamed him for joining with papal forces to assist Irish Catholics in defying English rule. Philip's power had been magnified recently when he asserted his claim to the throne of Portugal by invading that country. He now ruled one of the greatest empires in history. His trade routes and colonies circled the globe and were shielded by a navy six times the size of England's. But Drake had dramatically demonstrated the vulnerability of those trade routes, and other English mariners were sure to follow his lead.

Drake had embarked on his historic voyage in 1577 with the queen's tacit approval. After sailing down the west coast of Africa and targeting Spanish and Portuguese ships along the way, he crossed the Atlantic to South America and boldly threaded the treacherous Strait of Magellan at the base of the continent, buck-

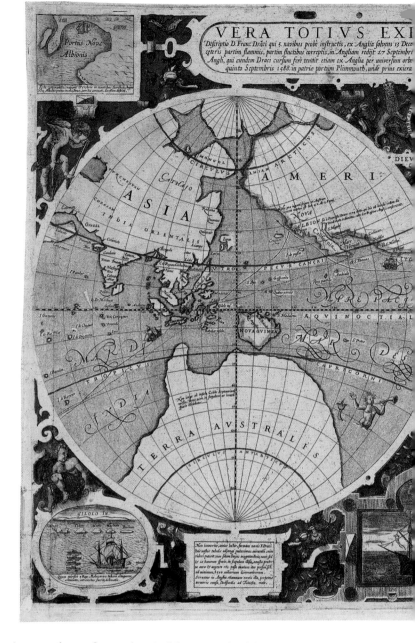

ing a gale so fierce that it felt to Drake like the very wrath of God. Having weathered that ordeal, he guided the *Golden Hind* up the west coast of the Americas to prey on Spanish merchantmen carrying treasure wrested from the land of the Incas and other subject peoples of the New World. Drake feared encountering fierce storms and Spanish warships if he returned through the Strait of Magellan, so he instead headed west across the vast Pacific, going 68 days without glimpsing land. He eventually

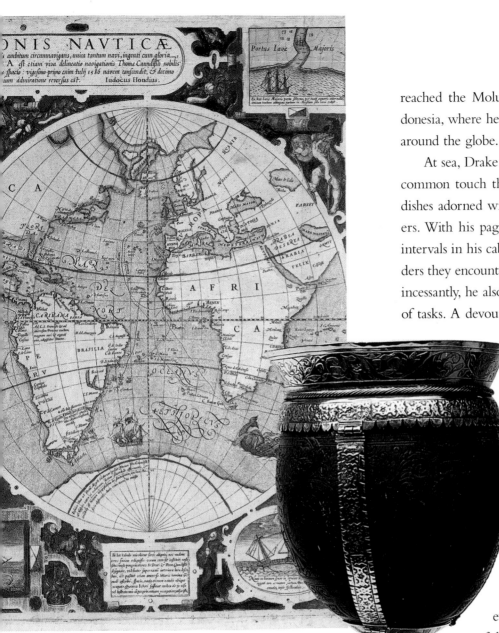

This map of Drake's circumnavigation, published not long after his return, traces the route of his ship, the *Golden Hind*, from England to Africa, across the sea, through the Strait of Magellan, up the west coast of the Americas, across the Pacific to the Spice Islands, and back home. He delighted Elizabeth by bringing her captured Spanish treasure as well as such exotic items as a coconut, which she had made into a commemorative goblet *(right)*.

reached the Moluccas, the fabled Spice Islands of present-day Indonesia, where he met with the sultan of Ternate before continuing around the globe.

At sea, Drake combined an acquired aristocratic manner with a common touch that endeared him to his crew. He dined on silver dishes adorned with his coat of arms while serenaded by viol players. With his page, his teenage cousin John Drake, he passed long intervals in his cabin painting the exotic birds, trees, and other wonders they encountered on their journey. Although he drilled his men incessantly, he also pitched in beside them to perform the humblest of tasks. A devout Protestant, he often spent several hours a day in worship and on Sunday led his crew in prayers and singing of psalms. But he trusted in his own gifts as much as he did in God's grace. "No one in the world," he boasted, "understood better the art of sailing."

Drake and his crew returned home in the fall of 1580 as the first Englishmen to circle the globe. In London, people swarmed about him in the streets. His name was known to friend and foe alike. The Spanish ambassador in London called him "the master-thief of the unknown world."

What the Spanish defined as thievery, however, the English defended as a legitimate assertion of their right to compete on the high seas for the spoils of distant lands. Although England's navy was small in comparison with Spain's, its merchant fleet was large and filled with enterprising captains and sailors who constituted a great asset in the emerging contest with Spain. Yet Elizabeth fully appreciated the risks of war with such a formidable power. To avoid open conflict, she preferred to challenge Philip through private ventures, whether of a predatory nature like Drake's or devoted to trade, exploration, or colonization. Even ventures that were ostensibly peaceful or went miserably awry, however, served to heighten tensions between England and Spain, propelling Elizabeth and her forces toward an epic confrontation with the Spanish fleet.

England's prospects in that momentous power struggle were greatly enhanced by the encouragement the queen offered to far-sighted commanders like Drake and his gifted colleague, Sir Walter Raleigh. These adventurers were driven to great feats not just by dreams of wealth and glory but by their devotion to Elizabeth and by their eagerness to justify her faith in them. They carried her hopes and prayers with them when they ventured abroad—and basked in her gratitude when they returned with their prizes.

Richard Madox seemed an unlikely applicant for adventure on the high seas. A 35-year-old native of Shropshire, he was an Anglican clergyman and a scholar and fellow at Oxford University. But his patron, Robert Dudley, the earl of Leicester—who first courted the queen as her Master of the Horse and now served as one of her Privy councilors and as chancellor of Oxford—was organizing a trading voyage to the Far East and had recommended that Madox serve as one of the expedition's two chaplains. So on this January day in 1582, Madox found himself in London's Muscovy House, headquarters for a prominent group of merchants, facing a panel of interviewers that included the celebrated Sir Francis Drake. They were satisfied with his credentials and pleased with his reply when asked what he expected in the way of remuneration. As Madox related, "I answered that I sought not gain but was glad to serve my country."

Such selflessness was appealing in a chaplain, but the sponsors themselves hoped to gain much by their investments. The expedition was intended as a follow-up to Drake's earlier visit with the sultan of Ternate in the Moluccas, which abounded in cloves, prized for making salted meat palatable and fresh meat more appetizing. For now at least, Elizabeth wanted to avoid pro-

voking Philip any further, so the men in command of the expedition were supposed to forsake plundering and confine themselves to trading. Unfortunately for the interests of peace, however, they would not be able to resist emulating Drake.

Drake himself was an investor in the expedition and an adviser to Leicester. Drake contributed nearly £700 as well as a small ship, the *Francis,* and recruited more than a dozen comrades from his epic voyage, including his cousin and former page, John Drake, now about 20 years old, who would captain the *Francis,* one of several vessels committed to the expedition.

The man originally chosen to lead the expedition was the accomplished Martin Frobisher, who had captained three voyages into Arctic waters. But for reasons that remained private, the crusty Frobisher was replaced at the last minute by one of his less gifted lieutenants on the Arctic voyages, Edward Fenton, more of a soldier than a sailor. Fenton was urged to avoid the Strait of Magellan, which the Spaniards would almost certainly fortify, and proceed instead around the Cape of Good Hope at the base of Africa and eastward to the Spice Islands.

On May 1, 1582, four months later than planned, Fenton's flotilla departed England. In addition to the *Francis* under John Drake, it included a small supply vessel, the *Elizabeth,* and two large warships, the *Galleon Leicester* and the *Edward Bonaventure,* each carrying more than 40 cannon to cope with any opposition that arose. Fenton himself served as captain of the *Galleon Leicester,* while his deputy, Luke Ward, had charge of the *Edward Bonaventure.* They were to endure what Ward would later describe with considerable understatement as "a troublesome voyage." In fact, the expedition would be a study in futility, demon-

Sir Francis Drake's warships menace the Spanish port of Santiago in the Cape Verde Islands in 1585, distracting the coastal batteries, while his soldiers advance on the town in tight ranks *(right)* and force the defenders out. Using similar tactics, Drake ravaged Spanish outposts in the New World, including St. Augustine in Florida.

strating how much English sea dogs still had to learn when it came to matching the Spaniards in the chase for distant riches.

Chronicling the misadventures was the observant chaplain Madox, aboard the *Galleon Leicester.* He served as official registrar and kept an account of the journey in that capacity, as well as a private diary, often recording his entries there in Latin, Greek, or a cipher of his own invention to shield his frequently scathing comments from prying eyes. He got on better with the ship's crew than with its officers. Many of the seamen were volunteers who had served with Drake or Frobisher; others had been impressed, or forced into service, by the queen's authority. In any case, their lot was a hard one, and Madox felt for them.

He did what he could to relieve the punishments meted out by Fenton and his subordinates. Madox recorded that under the great seal provided by the queen, Fenton had "absolute power and authority" to "order, rule, govern, correct and punish by imprisonment and violent means and by death." Tight discipline was necessary, of course. Food and drink had to be strictly rationed, and even the careless use of a candle risked fire and explosion. Among the punishments men faced on the journey was confinement to the bilboes—long bars with shackles for the feet. One officer was confined to the bilboes for speaking ill of Fenton at the mess table. Madox and his fellow chaplain, John Walker, aboard the *Edward Bonaventure,* interceded, and the punishment was cut short. Madox also appealed for mercy in the case of a carpenter's boy who stole a shirt and was hoisted to the yardarm in preparation for ducking in the sea. "I showed them that because we carried felonous harts," he wrote, "therefore God sent us felons among ourselves."

Rations were a constant worry on the voyage. Men blamed the food shortages on Martin Frobisher, who had been in charge of stocking the ships. "The sailors suppose, not wrongly," wrote Madox, "that there was a great cozenage in provisioning the journey and that he had profited much." When the fishing hooks of the sailors came up empty, Madox concluded that it was folly to go to sea without sufficient victuals, in the vain hope that flying fish might "break their noses against the bunt of the sail." To make matters worse, the ship ran out of London-brewed beer. "It seemed to all of us to be the very nectar of the gods," the chaplain wrote. Nor was fresh water in abundance, he noted, "owing to the decay of the casks, gaping with cracks."

Scurvy was the bane of this and many other voyages of the day. A few months into the voyage, chaplain Walker reported almost 40 men sick with scurvy: "It taketh them in their legs . . .

MARITIME JUSTICE

Unruly sailors in Elizabethan times faced a harrowing array of punishments of the sort portrayed at right. Captains tried to keep the peace by laying down rules of conduct like those spelled out by Drake's cousin, Sir John Hawkins: "Serve God duly, love one another, preserve your victuals, beware of fire, and keep good company."

But men who defied the captain or committed crimes received little mercy. "Just think," Drake asked a jury he convened on the *Golden Hind* to try a man accused of mutiny, "what would become of you if I were dead?" The jury pondered that prospect and condemned the man to death. Other offenders were punished with similar severity. Murderers were tied to the body of their victim and thrown overboard, anyone drawing a knife on an officer had his right hand cut off, and thieves were dunked three times into the sea and banished at next landfall.

the flesh becomes soft and swelleth in the knees . . . their teeth grow loose and their gums swell." When the expedition put in for repairs and fresh water at Sierra Leone, on the coast of west Africa, most of those with scurvy quickly recovered on a diet that included lemons. (It would be two centuries before the Royal Navy recognized the link between scurvy and a lack of fruit in the diet and issued lime juice daily, leading to the name "limey" for a British sailor.)

Madox had little faith in the expedition's doctor, John Banister, although the man was licensed by Oxford as both a physi-cian and a surgeon. His common remedy for fevers and most other ailments was the prevailing one of the time—letting blood. Madox himself had Banister let about 10 ounces from his left arm when he felt that his blood was "boiling with excessive heat." But he was not happy with the results, reporting that "mine arm hath been stiff there ever since." Madox concluded that since this doctor "had neither skill nor medicine," future expeditions should carry "good provision of wholesome comforts and ordinary salves and let them lie in the hands of some honest merchant."

Madox also looked askance at the ship's pilot, Thomas Hood.

The chaplain himself was versed in navigation and brought along his own book of astronomical tables and an instrument for measuring the height of the sun and stars. Navigators normally checked their position by sighting the sun at noon and then referring to the astronomical tables to establish their latitude. Such observations served to correct the pilot's dead reckoning, based on rough calculations of the ship's course and the distance traveled. But Hood thought that he could do without the books and tables other navigators relied on. "He will not give a fart for all their cosmography," Madox wrote, "for he can tell more than all the cosmographers in the world." As it turned out, Hood's self-confidence was unjustified. During a two-week period off west Africa when clouds prevented sightings of sun or stars, his dead reckoning proved dead wrong, and they traveled in a giant circle.

What disturbed Madox most of all was the talk of plundering. A few weeks after setting out, Fenton's flotilla apprehended a Flemish merchant ship off the coast of Portugal but let it go unmolested at the insistence of the two chaplains. The next day was a Sunday, and Madox preached against piracy, but his sermon did little to sway the would-be raiders, who argued that "we could not do God better service than to spoil the Spaniard both of life and goods." Fenton only encouraged such piratical ambitions. Madox heard tell that he wanted to set himself up as king of St. Helena, an island in the South Atlantic, with the crewmen as colonists. They would then seize the cargoes of Portuguese merchant vessels that watered there.

Madox in his diary lambasted Fenton as "our little king," bent on emulating Drake as "author of some great enterprise." Yet Fenton lacked Drake's gifts as a sailor and a commander. Distrust and dissension marked his relations with his officers and with the five merchants the sponsors had sent along. Major decisions were supposed to be made by a council that included the merchants, the chaplains, and some of the ships' officers, but Fenton excluded the tradesmen from most meetings.

Below, a master shipwright uses a compass to draw up plans for a vessel, aided by his young apprentice. English shipbuilders like those pictured laboring on the framework of a craft at left preferred to use hard, durable oak, which tested the strength of sawyers and carpenters.

Fenton evidently had little intention of following his instructions and found a ready excuse to avoid them. Faced with delays that prevented the expedition from reaching the Cape of Good Hope while the winds were still favorable, he instead sailed across the Atlantic toward the Strait of Magellan, where his instructions forbade him venturing "except upon great occasion incident." He had the council's backing in this, for much of his company wanted to follow Drake's course through the strait and up the west coast of South America to help themselves to Spanish treasure.

As Fenton had been warned, however, the Spanish were moving to fortify the strait. In early December, he received chilling confirmation of their plans from a Portuguese ship he captured off the coast of Brazil, whose passengers revealed that a Spanish fleet of at least 15 vessels was bound for the strait. Once again, Fenton convened a council and his ships changed course, abandoning the attempt to pass through the strait and heading instead for São Vicente on the Brazilian coast. Madox heard that Fenton was thinking of making himself king there and harvesting the cargoes of Portuguese ships. But the change of plan infuriated John Drake, who wanted to continue on through the strait and broke off from the expedition, leaving Fenton with just two ships (he had earlier bartered away the *Elizabeth* for much-needed rice and ivory). Shaken by Drake's defection, Fenton headed for São Vicente with the avowed purpose of engaging in "honest trading."

Whatever his intentions, Fenton received a frosty welcome when the two ships entered the harbor at São Vicente in January 1583. The Portuguese there, now under Spanish authority, refused to trade with the English, fearing the wrath of King Philip, who had forbidden such commerce after Drake's depredations. Soon three Spanish ships dispatched from the fleet bound for the Strait of Magellan entered the harbor. As Fenton noted dryly, they seemed deter-

mined "rather to fight with us, than to suffer us to rest in qui-
et there." Around 10:00 that night, the Spanish rode into battle on the incoming tide. In the ensuing fight, which raged
until 4:00 the next morning, Fenton's ship sank one of the
Spanish vessels. But he failed to capitalize on his success, reportedly because his men consumed a hogshead of wine and
were too drunk to continue the battle. As a result, their companion ship, captained by Luke Ward, had to fight alone for
four hours that day against the two surviving Spanish vessels.

Afterward, Ward and his crew separated from their
leader, arriving back in England in late May of 1583, a month
before Fenton. The disastrous venture had cost the lives of
more than one-third of the men, many of whom succumbed
to illness. Among the casualties was the intrepid chaplain and
chronicler, Richard Madox, who died of disease aboard Fenton's forlorn ship in February.

Sir Francis Drake, surveying the shambles of the mission
that was supposed to exploit his opening to the Far East, was
concerned most of all about his missing cousin, whose ship
had come to grief along the east coast of South America and
who was imprisoned by the Spanish, who held him captive
for the rest of his life. News of his fate reached Drake belat-
edly and did nothing to diminish his animus toward all things
Spanish. Indeed, the entire Fenton fiasco, conceived as a peaceful
alternative to plundering, served instead to increase tensions
and bring Elizabeth a small step closer to war with Philip.

Walter Raleigh suffered a loss of his own not long after
Drake's young cousin disappeared. In September 1583 Raleigh learned of the death of his elder half-brother, Sir
Humphrey Gilbert, lost at sea on the way home from an expedition to Newfoundland. Although not a great sailor or
commander, the farsighted Gilbert had recognized that England's hopes of becoming a great power depended on colo-

Two sailors with sounding leads, surrounded by
other nautical instruments, adorn the frontispiece of *The Mariners Mirrour,* a 16th-century
atlas and handbook of navigation.

A New Course for Science

Voyages to the New World and the Far East brought glory and wealth to England. They also helped bring about a sea change in scientific theory and practice. In time, such expeditions altered the way people viewed the world, filling out the map of the globe and greatly expanding the scientific roster of plants, animals, and peoples. More immediately, the urge to explore and exploit distant lands spurred major advances in the art of navigation and its related disciplines—astronomy, mathematics, and the design of better instruments for surveying the heavens and calculating a ship's position. Those who made these advances and applied them ceased to rely blindly on the teachings of medieval scholars or the ancients and charted a new course for scientific inquiry, based on observation and verification.

Chief among the men who helped bridge the gulf between those old schools of thought and the new science was Queen Elizabeth's royal astrologer, John Dee. Although astrology was an ancient and mystical art, Dee and others versed in its lore were keen surveyors of the heavens who kept up with the latest findings. Dee corresponded with the great Danish astronomer Tycho Brahe, acquired some of the finest astronomical instruments in Europe, and combined his talent for observation with a genius for mathematics to improve navigation.

An authority on Euclidean geometry, he applied mathematical principles to such problems as calculating a ship's position in waters near the poles, where pilots had to take into account the increased curvature of the earth. Dee had tremendous impact as an author and a teacher, instructing many English captains and pilots in navigation and enlightening promising young scholars. His students included men such as Thomas Digges, who helped popularize the Copernican view that the sun rather than the earth lay at the center of the cosmos, and Thomas Harriot, navigator and chief scientist for the voyage to colonize the New World organized by Sir Walter Raleigh in 1585.

Such expeditions led to discoveries in

Devised in 1569, this compendium combines several navigational aids, including a compass, a sundial, a nocturnal for sighting the polestar, and tables of latitudes and tides.

An illustration from 1576 shows the planets revolving around the sun, combining that new concept with the old idea of the stars as divine, "the very court of celestial angels."

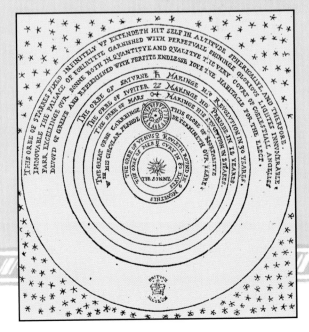

These tropical fish and a sea urchin were sketched by Richard Madox, a clergyman of wide scientific interests, in the journal he kept during a 1582 expedition organized by Robert Dudley.

Six varieties of irises are featured in John Gerard's 1597 botanical "history," containing some 1,800 illustrations as well as notes on the medicinal properties of various plants, some of which Gerard tended in his own gardens.

the natural world that were as useful as those being made by astronomers scanning the heavens. Seafaring naturalists like Harriot and Richard Madox, the chaplain who chronicled an ill-fated English expedition to the South Atlantic in 1582, added to the fund of knowledge about existing species and discovered new ones. This painstaking process of description and classification paid practical dividends by identifying animals and plants of commercial or medicinal value. In ven-

tures abroad, such information could spell the difference between success and failure. At home, it could lead to effective treatments for ills long thought to be incurable. In 1597 a barber-surgeon by the name of John Gerard published a meticulously illustrated encyclopedia of native and foreign plants, listing their medicinal properties. This herbal health guide became a bestseller and exemplifies the way in which scientific information gradually began to supplant folklore.

the flynge fish 180

echinos marinus
the sea vrchin

delphinos hispanice
Alberone.

nization and trade. Five years before his death, he had obtained from Elizabeth the right to establish the first English colony in North America. Raleigh picked up where Gilbert left off. By aggressively promoting the colonization of North America, he would fan England's smoldering dispute with Spain, which already had an outpost at St. Augustine in Florida and isolated forts and missions along the coast to the north.

At the time of Gilbert's death, Raleigh was about 30 and hungry for land and fortune. The youngest son of minor gentry in Drake's home county of Devonshire, he was a resourceful sailor and soldier, having served the queen as a captain in Ireland against papal mercenaries and Irish insurgents. Strikingly handsome and tall—he stood just over six feet at a time when the average male was more than a half-foot shorter—he had brooding eyes, dark hair, and a trim beard that accentuated his keen features. As if to flaunt his ambitions, he dressed richly in bright colors and flashing jewelry. He was "damnably proud," one contemporary observed, and so quick-tempered that he was twice imprisoned for brawling.

In seeking authorization from the queen to carry on his brother Gilbert's work, Raleigh had a special advantage. Since returning from Ireland in late 1581, he had become Elizabeth's favorite courtier—a distinction Leicester had forfeited when he married without the queen's blessing in 1578. Raleigh as yet had no wife to divert him from his devotion to Elizabeth, and reports of his gallantry toward her would become the stuff of legend. By the most famous account, he won her favor by throwing down his cloak in her path so that she would not get her royal feet wet. Another colorful anecdote portrayed him as a lovelorn poet who wooed Elizabeth by using the diamond in his ring to scrawl a line on a windowpane—"Fain would I climb, yet I fear to fall"—to which she reportedly replied underneath, "If thy heart fail thee, climb not at all." Whatever the truth of these tales, Elizabeth was genuinely captivated by this eloquent adventurer, who was young enough to be her son. Her cherished reputation as the Virgin Queen did not prevent her from pursuing an innocent love affair with a courtier who embodied her ideals of masculine grace, courage, and wit.

In March 1584, six months after learning of his brother's death,

Raleigh was granted a similar patent by Elizabeth to colonize North America, authorizing him to occupy "countries and territories not actually possessed of any Christian Prince." Raleigh thus had wide latitude in choosing a site for his colony, and the patent gave him broad powers once he established it, subject only to payment to the queen of one-fifth of any gold or silver mined there. Once equipped with his patent, he sent off a two-ship mission to reconnoiter the east coast of North America and began preparing for a major expedition.

Raleigh settled himself in rooms reserved for him by the queen in the palatial Durham House, overlooking the Thames. Among those he recruited to assist him was Thomas Harriot, a brilliant young scientist and mathematician from Oxford, who set up shop on the top floor of Durham House and did all he could to ensure that the leaders of Raleigh's planned expedition had the benefit of what Fenton, for one, had sorely lacked—expert navigation. Harriot took observations from the roof and devised new instruments and techniques. He also conducted classes in navigation for Raleigh's pilots, masters, and captains. Raleigh himself attended, mindful of his brother's misfortune at sea.

Hoping to win financial backing as well from Elizabeth, Raleigh mounted a propaganda offensive. He asked his friend, Richard Hakluyt, a young clergyman serving as chaplain and secretary to the English ambassador in Paris, to return to London and prepare a treatise for the queen on the benefits of colonizing North America. Hakluyt, who had spoken with veterans of French expeditions to the New World, painted a glowing picture of a vigorous English colony in North America that would serve as a base for attacks against the Spaniards and export to the homeland such valuable goods as wine, olive oil, gold, and silver.

Raleigh saw to it that the scouts he had sent off to the New World confirmed Hakluyt's optimistic view in their report when they returned. On the island of Roanoke, off the mainland of present-day North Carolina, they had encountered native people

"most gentle, loving and faithful, void of all guile and treason." English peas planted there shot up 14 inches in just 10 days in soil that "is the most plentiful, sweet, fruitful and wholesome of all the world." The expedition also brought back two Indians, Manteo and Wanchese, who willingly made the journey and instructed Thomas Harriot in their Algonquian language. Raleigh dressed the two Indians in brown taffeta in the English fashion and introduced them to the queen. Elizabeth was entranced, and these visitors from another world became the toast of London.

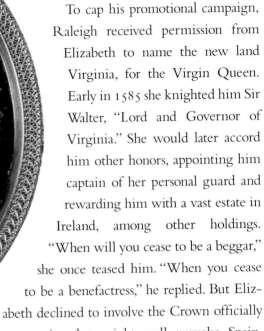

Sir Walter Raleigh *(right)* fared better at promoting his Virginia colony than at selecting its site. Encouraged by scouting reports, he chose Roanoke Island *(below left)*, off the coast of present-day North Carolina. But the area was plagued by sudden, violent storms and treacherous sand bars and became a graveyard for ships, shown littering the coast in this map by colonist John White.

Pasquenoke

WEAPEMEOC

Trinety harbor

To cap his promotional campaign, Raleigh received permission from Elizabeth to name the new land Virginia, for the Virgin Queen. Early in 1585 she knighted him Sir Walter, "Lord and Governor of Virginia." She would later accord him other honors, appointing him captain of her personal guard and rewarding him with a vast estate in Ireland, among other holdings. "When will you cease to be a beggar," she once teased him. "When you cease to be a benefactress," he replied. But Elizabeth declined to involve the Crown officially in an enterprise that might well provoke Spain. Raleigh had her blessing, and she even granted him the use of a royal ship. But the expedition would have to make do with the funds Raleigh had raised from his own purse and from investors.

It would also have to make do without Raleigh. To his shock and disappointment, Elizabeth decided that she could not spare her favorite courtier. Raleigh entrusted command of the expedition to his relative, Sir Richard Grenville. A fiery soldier named Ralph Lane would have charge of the colonists once they went ashore at Roanoke Island. In April 1585 a half-dozen ships carrying 600 men—100 of whom would be left on the island as settlers—sailed out of Plymouth harbor. Thomas Harriot went along to supervise navigation and serve the colonists as chief scientist, naturalist, and liaison with the Indians.

A few months later, while Raleigh fretted over the fate of his venture, Drake organized an even larger expedition—this one aimed directly at Spanish interests in the New World. Elizabeth threw caution aside and authorized Drake's warlike foray in response to a provocative embargo imposed by King Philip that resulted in the seizure of English merchant ships and crews delivering desperately needed grain to Spanish ports.

In September 1585 the newly commissioned Admiral Drake set out with a formidable flotilla of more than two dozen ships and at least 2,300 men. His first objective was to free the English ships and crews in Spanish ports, but he soon learned that the embargo had been lifted and so turned to his second assignment—to take reprisals against King Philip's subjects by pillaging them wherever he deemed fit. He swept across the Atlantic, striking first at the Spanish in the Cape Verde Islands before sacking Santo Domingo in the West Indies, Cartagena on the northeastern coast of South America, and St. Augustine in Florida. After picking that outpost clean, the admiral and his men sailed up the coast with their booty to aid Raleigh's colonists at Roanoke.

Drake arrived there with his flotilla in June 1586 and found the settlers famished and demoralized. They had lost most of their provisions when one of their ships struck a shoal as they neared the island a year earlier, and by then it had been too late for them to plant crops. Nor had they gleaned much in the way of riches from the land, although the region contained some things of interest to the English, including pearls and the potent native tobacco, which Harriot, for one, found invigorating, reporting that it "openeth all the pores and passages of the body." For subsistence, the colonists relied on trade with the Indians, who at first welcomed the newcomers but in time grew scornful of men who seemed woefully unable to provide for themselves.

Finally, just one week before Drake arrived, Ralph Lane concluded that the Indians were about to attack and launched a preemptive strike against the leading chieftain that left the colonists isolated and vulnerable to reprisals. In the end, they returned to England with Drake, whose men departed the storm-racked coast in such haste that they left behind three settlers and some of the colonists' belongings, including a string of pearls that Lane had hoped to present to Queen Elizabeth.

The place of solemne prayer.

Their sitting at

The house wherin the Tombe of their Herounds standeth.

SECOTO

As portrayed by John White, the Algonquians lived in well-tended villages like Secotan *(left)* and were expert bowmen and skilled planters. Thomas Harriot marveled that they raised corn without "muck, dung, or any other thing," unaware that beans planted with the corn fertilized the stalks at their roots.

Raleigh was sorely disappointed by the failure of his venture, but he continued to promote the colonization of Virginia, amusing the queen by puffing on a silver pipe filled with tobacco. He would soon dispatch a second group of colonists to the region, this one made up of women as well as men. But those hard-pressed settlers would vanish from Roanoke Island, never to be heard from again, and nearly two decades would elapse before the English established an enduring colony in Virginia. In the short term, the chief consequence of Raleigh's bold initiative—and Drake's blistering foray—was to goad Spain by breaching the defenses of its sprawling New World empire. As Drake announced proudly after returning from his venture, "There is now a very great gap opened, very little to the liking of the King of Spain."

Philip could not let such challenges from Elizabeth go unanswered. In addition to authorizing Drake's expedition, she had recently affirmed by treaty her support for the Dutch Protestants rebelling against Spanish authorities and committed English troops to that contest. She no longer cared to disguise such hostile maneuvers, and Philip was prepared to respond in kind by invading England and toppling her—with or without help from restive English Catholics. The execution of Mary, Queen of Scots, ended Spanish hopes of ousting Elizabeth through subterfuge even as it spurred Philip to proceed with plans for an invasion, led by one of the greatest armadas ever to sail the high seas.

Those elaborate naval preparations were soon detected by English agents abroad, and Drake implored the queen to let him strike the first blow, before the Armada could gather. Elizabeth hesitated, still hoping that war might somehow be averted, but she concluded at last that conflict was inevitable and authorized Drake "to impeach the purpose of the Spanish threat." He embarked in early April of 1587 with some two dozen ships. Ten days later, the queen had second thoughts and tried to call him back, but it was too late. On April 19, her golden knight and company rode insolently into the Spanish port of Cádiz with cannon blazing and burned or sank more than 25 vessels. Subsequently, he destroyed shiploads of hoops and other materials needed to make the casks that would carry the Armada's food and water. Then he made a dash for the Azores, leading the Spanish on a wild-goose chase and capturing a ship containing cargo worth more than £100,000. With unaccustomed modesty, Drake remarked that he had done no more than "singe the King of Spain's beard." In fact, he had so disrupted their preparations that the invasion had to be postponed until 1588.

The delay gave the English time to get ready. The Royal Navy had at its disposal only 34 fighting ships, but the Crown swelled the fleet to some 200 vessels by enlisting the services of privately owned craft. Some of those vessels were suited only for auxiliary duties like scouting or carrying supplies, and they would not all be gathered in one place, but the enlarged fleet still represented a stiff challenge for the vaunted Armada of some 130 ships the Spanish were assembling. Following tradition, Elizabeth had selected a nobleman to command the fleet—her cousin, Charles Howard, Lord Effingham. At age 52, the Lord High Admiral was untested in battle, but he knew the sea and compensated for his shortcomings by listening to Drake, who served as vice-admiral.

Raleigh, for his part, helped in several ways to prepare the realm for the looming confrontation. He served on the queen's council of war, contributed two of his own ships to the fleet, and as lord lieutenant for Cornwall oversaw the mustering and arming of the local militia. Across England, tens of thousands of militiamen were placed on alert. Nearly 17,000 gathered at Tilbury Camp, not far from London, to defend the capital against invaders. More than 20,000 others formed a kind of mobile reserve in maritime counties such as Cornwall and prepared to meet the enemy at potential landing places. They would be warned by a system of beacons—braziers sited on hilltops and filled with tar-soaked brushwood that would be ignited at the approach of Spanish ships.

All through the late spring and early summer of 1588, Drake expected those beacons to flare up at any time. But mishaps and delays beset Philip's grand Armada. First, his commander died, forcing Philip to recruit a reluctant replacement, the duke of Medina-Sidonia. Possessed of considerable wealth and great skill at fitting out fleets bound for the New World, Medina-Sidonia protested that he had no experience commanding ships and was prone to seasickness. But he was a religious man, and he duly consented to lead the Invincible Armada, as the pope christened the fleet, on what Philip regarded as a holy crusade.

Shortly after the Armada set sail from Lisbon in May, a terrific storm scattered the ships. Not until mid-July did the fleet approach the broad mouth of the English Channel, south of Cornwall. Medina-Sidonia's plan was to avoid battle if possible and proceed northeastward to the narrow Strait of Dover to provide protection for the principal invasion force, a powerful 17,000-man army from the Netherlands under Philip's nephew, the duke of Parma. Those battle-tested men were to cross the strait on boats and barges, disembark on England's eastern coast, and march for London, while the Armada sailed up the Thames to guard their flank.

Howard and Drake, for their part, hoped to intercept and disrupt the Armada before it could menace their ports or their capital. On Friday, July 19, they were in Plymouth harbor with the bulk of the fleet when word arrived in midafternoon that a scouting vessel had spotted "many ships of great burden" off the southern tip of Cornwall—a point known as The Lizard, situated roughly 60 miles southwest of Plymouth. It would take time for the fleet to respond. To exit Plymouth, the English had to await nightfall and the ebb tide, and even then, the wind was against them and progress was painfully slow.

By Sunday morning, July 21, most of the ships had cleared Plymouth harbor and were arrayed for battle in two squadrons, one at either flank of the advancing Armada. To take advantage

An angel offers King Philip II of Spain a laurel wreath in this portrait by the Flemish master Peter Paul Rubens. A devout ruler whose palace grounds, the Escorial, included a church and monastery, Philip claimed God's blessing in his campaign to crush Elizabeth and restore England to the Catholic faith.

of the wind, Howard and Drake had positioned their squadrons slightly behind the opposing fleet and would content themselves with harrying the Spanish—a prudent decision in light of the fearsome prospect confronting them. Arrayed in a crescent more than two miles wide, the Armada enjoyed superiority in numbers—125 vessels compared to the 105 Howard and Drake had available for this battle—and in sheer bulk. One witness marveled at the towering Spanish warships, "with lofty turrets like castles," and noted that they advanced "very slowly, though with full sails, the winds being as it were tired of carrying them, and the ocean groaning under the weight of them."

Those hulking warships, with their high forecastles, were designed as platforms for boarding enemy ships. If their captains succeeded in bringing them near enough to the English for that purpose, the Spanish would then be able to exert their huge advantage in manpower—the Armada carried more than 17,000 troops, compared with just 1,500 aboard the English vessels. On the other hand, the English had a decided edge when it came to maneuvering and dueling. The Armada included many cumbersome merchant ships, weighed down with troops, horses, and ordnance for the invasion, and their ponderous pace slowed the fleet. And the trim English warships not only were faster and nimbler than

their Spanish counterparts but also exceeded them in firepower.

Howard and Drake used those assets to jab at their weighty foes while keeping a respectful distance. With the wind at their backs, the English swept around either flank of the Armada, raking the enemy ships with gunfire from afar for some four hours. "We durst not adventure to put in among them," conceded Howard, "their fleet being so strong." Although this opening round in the struggle for control of England amounted to little more than a skirmish, the Spanish suffered two significant mishaps after the fighting ended. One of their warships caught fire and its gunpowder exploded, killing some 200 men. A sec-

ond, the *Rosario,* bristling with 52 guns and loaded with gold ducats, was crippled when it collided with another Spanish ship. Ever on the lookout for loot, Drake and his flagship *Revenge* overtook the disabled *Rosario* during the night and forced its surrender. In gentlemanly fashion, Drake welcomed the Spanish commander aboard with trumpets and a banquet while his men seized the treasure.

Drake's lucrative coup left him open to criticism. He had been designated that night to lead the ships in pursuit of the Spanish, with a large lantern at the stern of the *Revenge* pointing the way. His detour to capture the *Rosario* threw the fleet into

English ships patrol the Dorset coast expectantly while flaming beacons alert distant militiamen of the approach of the Spanish Armada. The first sighting of that great war fleet, off the southern tip of Cornwall on July 19, 1588, ended months of suspense during which guards stood watch on promontories day and night and vessels scouted tirelessly for the enemy at sea.

turmoil. But if some faulted Drake for causing a distraction, others were simply envious of his haul. The quarrelsome Martin Frobisher, now serving as a captain in the fleet, threatened that if Drake failed to share the booty, "I will make him spend the best blood in his belly." Drake heard this secondhand and let it pass.

In the days to come, Drake and his colleagues pursued the Armada and did battle with the Spanish more than once but failed to halt their progress up the Channel. Then on Saturday, July 27, the Armada anchored off the neutral French port of Calais, across the strait from the English port of Dover. The Spanish hoped to rendezvous promptly with the invasion force from the Netherlands under the duke of Parma. But Medina-Sidonia learned to his horror that Parma's barges had been bottled up in the canals some 25 miles away by Dutch rebel ships and could not join him for days.

While Medina-Sidonia waited impatiently, Howard hastily gathered his forces and prepared to attack. After summoning a squadron that was patrolling nearby to prevent the crossing by Parma, he had 140 ships at his disposal. To pave the way for the assault, the English resorted to a familiar naval stratagem. On Sunday night, July 28, men loaded eight small ships with tar, twigs, and gunpowder, maneuvered them into position to ride the current and wind toward the anchored enemy, and set the vessels aflame before jumping overboard. Six of those fire ships got through a screen of small boats the Spanish had deployed to block them and barreled into the fleet, forcing most of the ships to hurriedly cut loose their anchor cables and disperse. They left behind their commander in his flagship, the *San Martin,* surrounded by four other vessels. At dawn, Medina-Sidonia headed out with those few ships to rejoin and reassemble his scattered Armada—and ran straight into the attacking English.

For Drake, who was leading the assault while Howard busied himself with capturing a Spanish warship that had run aground, the sight of the exposed *San Martin* must have been intoxicating. His ships swept in for the kill, closing to point-blank range and blasting away. Medina-Sidonia, untested at sea before the campaign, proved his mettle now by standing fast and absorbing the punishment to give the rest of his Armada time to re-form and respond. His *San Martin* took 200 shots in the

Following the first clash between the opposing fleets near Plymouth harbor on July 21, the Spanish Armada continues on its way in its protective crescent formation *(far right).* The Spanish left behind the disabled *Rosario (with severed mast at lower left),* which was then snared by Sir Francis Drake in his *Revenge.*

To protect themselves during combat, the English wore heavy vests such as this jack of plate, made of canvas lined with mail and reinforced underneath with overlapping plates of iron.

starboard side alone, and the smoke was so thick he had to make a perilous climb up the rigging to view the battle unfolding. Remarkably, the *San Martin* remained afloat, but her companion ships and other vessels of the Armada that rushed to their aid took a terrible beating. Blood flowed from the crowded upper decks. Four Spanish ships foundered and at least 1,000 Spanish soldiers and sailors died that day before the English ran out of shot and broke off the contest after nine hours.

The battle proved to be decisive. In the aftermath, the wind carried the battered Armada up into the North Sea, beyond the planned meeting with the duke of Parma, whose troops never reached English soil. Medina-Sidonia had little choice in the end

but to abandon the campaign and sail home with his fleet circuitously around Scotland and Ireland. Along the way, storms wrecked dozens of his ships, leaving the once-mighty Armada to limp home with nearly 50 percent losses.

Ten days after the crucial battle off Calais, Queen Elizabeth traveled down the Thames to visit the militiamen encamped at Tilbury. She had reason to be optimistic, but the English could not be certain as yet that the invasion had been thwarted. As she rode on her gray gelding among the cheering troops, she wore silver armor plate over her white gown and carried a truncheon, exuding the defiant spirit that carried her forces to victory. "I know I have the body of a weak and feeble woman," she told them, "but I have the heart and stomach of a king, and of a king of England too, and think foul scorn that Parma or Spain, or any prince of Europe should dare to invade the borders of my realm."

The defeat of the Armada left Spanish treasure ships all the more vulnerable to English raids. In May 1592, Sir Walter Raleigh, hoping to bolster his fortunes after meeting with little success in Virginia, led a 13-ship expedition out to sea to prey on the Spanish. Raleigh had been gone only a day, however, when he was overtaken by a vessel carrying Frobisher, who had an unwelcome message for Raleigh from the queen. The expedition could proceed under Frobisher's command, but Raleigh must return to England.

It was not the first time that Elizabeth had prevented Raleigh from venturing abroad. But on this occasion, she did so not with clinging affection but with cold fury, having discovered that Raleigh had deceived her by secretly marrying one of her attendants, a match he had kept hidden for some time while professing devotion to the queen. Elizabeth was in no mood to forgive either Raleigh or his bride—the vivacious Bess Throckmorton, daughter of the late ambassador to Scotland and France—and consigned the pair to separate quarters in the Tower.

After less than two months there, Raleigh was released on parole. He owed his freedom not to the letters he wrote protesting his devotion to her but to a crisis that demanded his urgent attention. The expedition he had organized and briefly commanded had succeeded almost too handsomely. Off the coast of Spain, the English had snared an enormous seven-deck Portuguese ship, the *Madre de Dios*. Its cargo from the East Indies was almost beyond belief, consisting of 537 tons of spices and 15 tons of ebony, along with countless pearls, diamonds, silks, and other valuables. The crewmen who boarded it had immediately begun stuffing their pockets, and the pillaging resumed when the ship reached Dartmouth harbor. The lure of spices and gems attracted merchants, jewelers, and goldsmiths, who descended on

In this Dutch painting, un-
manned English fire ships
(background) ride the
wind and tide toward the
Spanish fleet anchored off
Calais on the evening of
July 28—a tactic that scattered the Armada and left
it ill prepared for the decisive battle that erupted
the next morning. As one
Spaniard ruefully observed,
"With eight ships they put
us to flight, a thing they
had dared not to attempt
with a hundred and thirty."

143

the port to purchase plunder from sailors at a bargain. Raleigh's task was to stop the looting and protect the queen's profits.

Sailors greeted him at Dartmouth with cheers and shouts of joy. Raleigh told them he was still "the Queen of England's poor captive" and set to work with manic energy. He recovered most of the losses from the cargo, officially estimated to be worth £141,000. The queen claimed as her share more than half of that, far more than her actual investment. Some of what she garnered came at Raleigh's expense, who though nominally entitled to at least two-thirds of the loot, had to settle for about one-fourth. By succeeding in the rescue, however, he ceased to be the queen's poor captive and won freedom for his wife as well. Raleigh ultimately resumed his duties as captain of the queen's guard.

Even before his secret marriage came to light, Raleigh had been eclipsed as the queen's favorite by a much younger adventurer, Robert Devereux, the earl of Essex, who aside from being a nobleman had the advantage of being Leicester's stepson. In 1587, around the age of 20, Essex had been appointed by Elizabeth to succeed his stepfather as her Master of the Horse. By the time of Leicester's death the following year, the young nobleman had clearly emerged as the courtier the queen cared for most.

Tall and auburn haired, Essex was Raleigh's match in looks, though not in attire, little caring how his attendants dressed him. Not surprisingly, he and Raleigh rubbed each other the wrong way, and only the queen's intervention prevented a duel between the two courtiers. In 1596, when tensions with Spain once again reached the flash point and another invasion appeared imminent, Essex led an expedition to forestall that possibility, capturing and briefly holding the Spanish port of Cádiz. As a member of the Privy Council, he became Elizabeth's unofficial minister of war.

All this success before the age of 30 seemed to spoil him. He was given to sulking and wild suspicions. His tantrums and acts of defiance would enrage Elizabeth. Then, like a doting mother with a temperamental child, she would forgive all. Even when he

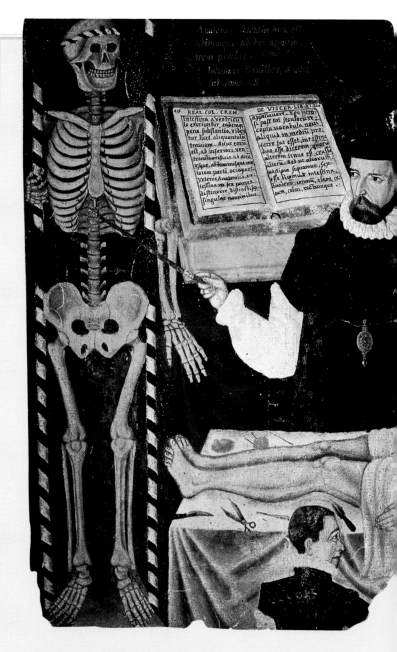

Surgeon and physician John Banister lectures in 1581 with the aid of a skeleton and a cadaver. Anatomical knowledge greatly increased after Henry VIII allowed dissections.

The Healing Profession

In an age of chronic pestilence and rampant infection, when most people died before the age of 50, ailing Elizabethans were willing to try almost any cure. Chicanery remained prevalent, and potion-peddling humbugs known as quacksalvers—or quacks, for short—did a brisk business. At the same time, however, the art of medicine was slowly developing into a science, thanks in part to advances in the treatment of men who had been wounded in battle and to lessons learned from the dissection of executed felons.

Among the healers in Elizabethan times were so-called wise women, or "witches," who generally offered treatment to other women. The regular medical profession consisted of three tiers, with physicians at the top, followed by surgeons and apothecaries. Physicians

Queen Mary lays hands on a young victim of scrofula, known as the king's evil because tradition held that it could be cured by the touch of a monarch.

Surgeon William Clowes *(left)* became an authority in his field by treating countless war wounds with instruments of the sort depicted amid the battlefield scenes above, in an illustration from one of his books.

were university trained, often on the Continent at places like Padua in Italy and Montpellier in France, but their healing skills were limited. They had little contact with patients, commonly confining their practice to a wealthy few, and remained devoted to Galen, a gifted Greek doctor of the second century AD whose teachings had become sacrosanct and were now hindering the progress of medicine. In the 1600s, for example, the English physician William Harvey conclusively demonstrated that, contrary to Galen's view, blood circulates to and from the heart—a finding that some of Harvey's colleagues rejected.

While physicians concerned themselves with theory, surgeons attended to more practical matters. They treated wounds, lanced boils, set broken bones, and amputated diseased and damaged limbs. Their skills were "not learned in the study," wrote the greatest surgeon of the day, Frenchman Ambroise Paré, but perfected in practice "by the eye and by the hands." The surgeon's laboratory was often the battlefield, where the recent introduction of gunpowder caused wounds that frequently required amputation.

Long experience in treating war wounds led English surgeons to improve their techniques and share their advances with colleagues in surgical manuals. In 1596, for example, surgeon William Clowes, who had operated on men wounded in battles against the Spanish Armada, offered the first account in English of the beneficial practice of tying off blood vessels during amputations instead of cauterizing them with hot metal or boiling pitch. Yet even the astute Clowes clung to folklore. In describing one case, he wrote that the injured man was in particular danger for having "received his hurt very near the full of the moon."

Those at the lowest rung of the medical system—the apothecaries who dispensed drugs and herbal remedies—were perhaps even more prone to such misconceptions. While some apothecaries were quacks, however, others outdid physicians at treating common ailments. To relieve headache, for example, they often prescribed willow-bark tea, containing a natural

analgesic. Most Elizabethans had no other choice but to trust in apothecaries—by one estimate, there was only one physician for every 25,000 people. English law recognized the need for folk medicine while seeking to bring it under some control. One ordinance allowed any person with a knowledge of herbal remedies to treat patients with minor ailments, but another authorized physicians to inspect the potions such apothecaries prepared.

A 16th-century surgeon amputates a man's leg without the benefit of anesthesia. Skilled surgeons could remove a limb while spilling as little as four ounces of the patient's blood.

married without her permission, she welcomed him back to court after a mere fortnight.

One summer day in 1598, however, Essex went too far. He and the queen were debating a matter of state when Essex lost his temper. In a gesture of contempt, he turned his back on his sovereign. Elizabeth responded by slapping him hard on the side of the head and urging him to be gone and hanged. In a flash, his hand flew to his sword. Lord High Admiral Howard jumped in to restrain him, but Essex stormed out, yelling that he would not have abided such treatment even from her father, Henry VIII. He returned to court after three months, with scarcely an apology, and found his relationship with the queen forever altered.

Elizabeth continued to rely on Essex, however. In 1599 she called upon him to lead a 16,000-man army to troubled Ireland—the largest English force ever sent there. He was ordered to subdue the rebels led by the mighty earl of Tyrone, whose vast holdings included 120,000 milk cows. Tyrone commanded an army of some 17,000 men, including as many as 6,000 Irish and Scottish mercenaries. After landing at Dublin, Essex defied his orders by marching south to deal with lesser rebels instead of heading north to challenge Tyrone in his Ulster stronghold. The queen rebuked Essex in writing for disobedience, but Essex was uncontrite, blaming her displeasure on enemies at court. "From England I have received nothing but discomforts and soul's wounds," he complained.

When Essex finally confronted Tyrone in September 1599, he chose to negotiate a six-week truce with the man he had been sent to subdue. After receiving a scathing letter from Elizabeth, Essex rushed back to court to defend himself. Mud-splattered from the journey, he barged into the queen's bedchamber at midmorning unannounced and found her barely dressed, without wig, makeup, or jewels, a gray-haired woman of 66, bereft of her regal trappings. He fell to his knee and kissed her hands. She smiled indulgently, but Essex was soon placed under house arrest and later charged with incompetence and disobedience. After his release, his relations with the queen went from bad to worse. In 1600, some £16,000 in debt, he begged Elizabeth to renew a lease entitling him to customs on imported sweet wines—his principal

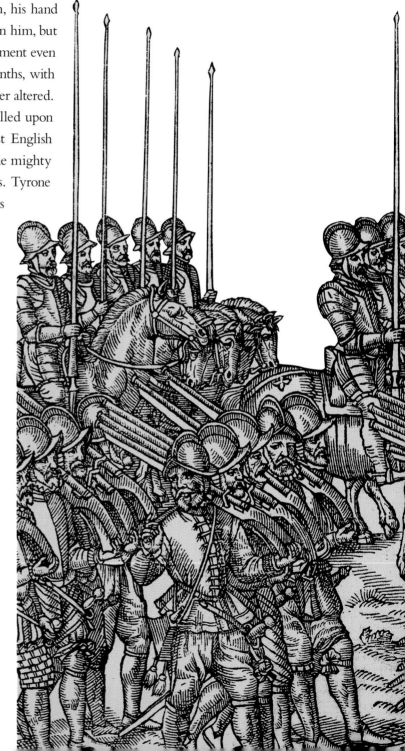

Bristling with pikes, muskets, and swords, an English army marches through Ireland. After Irish rebels repulsed English forces in 1598, Elizabeth appointed her former favorite, Robert Devereux, the earl of Essex *(left),* to put down the revolt. His failure earned him Elizabeth's lasting scorn and set the stage for his desperate attempt to seize power.

source of income. She refused, likening him to an unruly horse that would be easier to manage once "abated of his provender."

Essex could not tolerate such chastisement and soon hatched a plot against the queen and her advisers, including Raleigh. Joining Essex were other disaffected aristocrats who had squandered their fortunes and hoped to profit by the coup. Their goal was not necessarily to depose Elizabeth but to seize control of the court and have their way. Yet however much they protested their loyalty, their plot amounted to treason. Essex and his confederates seemed to signal as much in February of 1601 when they arranged for a special performance at the Globe Theatre of Shakespeare's *Richard II*—including the prohibited scene portraying the monarch's overthrow.

The next day, Raleigh learned of the plot from a cousin close to Essex and hastened back to court to sound the alarm. A few hours later, Essex and as many as 300 followers rode through the streets of London, trying to muster support by claiming implausibly that they were rising up to protect the queen from Raleigh

and other villains at court. Londoners, ever faithful to Elizabeth, turned a deaf ear to their appeals. That night, loyalists under Howard arrested Essex, who was quickly found guilty of treason and executed. Afterward, the executioner, adhering to grim custom, held up the severed head by the hair and shouted, "God save the Queen!"

The fall of Essex cast a pall over Elizabeth's final years. She often slipped into melancholy, lamenting her misfortunes. "She walks much in her Privy Chamber," noted her godson, John Harington, "and stamps with her feet at ill news." In fits of rage, she sometimes grabbed an old sword she kept at her bedside and thrust it into the draperies. But her strength was ebbing, and Harington could not help noticing that "our dear queen," though portrayed by artists as forever young, "doth now bear show of human infirmity." In March 1603, at the age of 69, she grew feverish and resigned herself to her fate, refusing food and medicine. "It seems she might have lived if she would have used means," wrote the aspiring lawyer John Manningham after speaking with her doctor, "but she would not be persuaded, and princes must not be forced."

Before she died in the early hours of March 24, Elizabeth acknowledged as her successor Mary Stuart's son, James, thus ensuring that England would remain Protestant. But what mattered most to Elizabeth in the end was not the succession or the Protestant cause but simply the fact that her nation endured and that the people to whom she had dedicated herself now inhabited a realm prouder and sturdier than the one she inherited. She had preserved and enhanced that precious inheritance in the face of fierce challenges at home and abroad, showing this "mere woman," as she put it, had a heart as strong as any king's.

Honor guards displaying the queen's coats of arms escort Elizabeth's coffin, topped by her effigy and pulled by black-draped horses, to Westminster Abbey. An artist later pictured her sepulcher there *(left)*, attended by a solitary mourner representing all her grieving subjects.

In a stunning display of wealth, Queen Elizabeth, shown here midway through her reign, is clothed in her nation's riches. The exquisite embroidery, gold lace, and bejeweled velvet bodice and skirt of her ensemble, as well as the clusters of diamonds and rubies and the strands of pearls, all reflect England's rising status as a world power.

Splendor Befitting a Queen

As the embodiment of her nation's power and status, Queen Elizabeth delighted in arraying herself in clothing and jewelry in keeping with England's burgeoning prosperity. During her reign, English merchant vessels—and privateers—ventured farther afield and brought home more gold and luxury goods than ever before. Elizabeth—and in their turn, the English nobility and rising merchant class—had access to the finest fabrics and jewels in all the world. They eagerly made use of this finery, ushering in one of the greatest and most colorful periods of English costume.

Managing Elizabeth's wardrobe was no mean feat. A veritable army was employed in the crafting, care, inventory, and storage of the queen's garments and jewels. The Keeper, or Master of the Great Wardrobe, oversaw the work of dozens of officials and artificers who purchased and crafted the bales of fabric, furs, ribbons, and lace used to make the queen's clothing and robes of state, as well as liveries for more than 200 yeomen, grooms, and pages in Elizabeth's court. Clerks of the Wardrobe kept meticulous records detailing how every shilling was spent. Through careful management and judicious alterations of existing gowns, the queen kept her clothing expenses under control. In fact, annual expenses for her clothing in the last four years of her reign were £9,525—a pittance compared with the £36,377 spent in one year by her successor, James I.

A good portion of this budget went toward luxurious fabrics. Even though the queen was a staunch protector of the English woolen industry (she assented to Parliament's law in 1571 that all commoners over age six must wear a cap made of wool, not velvet, on Sundays and holidays), she felt no compunction about purchasing for herself the best the world had to offer. Italian manufacturers produced the finest in figured damasks, brocades, and velvets, as well as gold and silver metallic lace. Linen was imported from Germany and the Low Countries. Silks woven with gold and silver strands came from Spain, as did sumptuous leathers for slippers and gloves. And gold, pearls, diamonds, rubies, and emeralds from India, Persia, and the New World were fashioned into ornaments sewn directly onto her gowns or made into royal necklaces, armlets, brooches, and crowns.

A 16th-century woodcut shows the bustle of activity in a typical goldsmith's shop. In addition to making jewelry for their affluent customers, goldsmiths in Elizabethan England were kept busy crafting insignia for state officials.

153

In Pursuit of Style

Visitors to Elizabeth's court were awed by the fabulous clothes worn by the queen and her courtiers, but some criticized the practice of wearing the styles of other countries instead of developing a distinctively English manner of dress. Critics at home and abroad called England "the ape of all nations" in matters of fashion, citing the habit of the fanciest dressers—including the queen—to wear Spanish, French, Italian, and Moorish styles, all within a single week.

But fashion was closely linked with economic prosperity, and Spain, as the most powerful European nation, established the basic style of dress for men and women of rank in late-16th-century Europe. The farthingale, a stiffened underskirt that supported women's gowns, was a Spanish invention adopted throughout Europe. English and French clothiers adapted the styles of Spain to their customers' tastes, however, rejecting the dark, somber dress colors preferred by the Spanish court in favor of brighter colors and a little décolletage.

Although she did not want the French court to know of her preference, Queen Elizabeth was particularly fond of their fashions and asked her chief adviser, Sir William Cecil, to find her a French tailor. Cecil wrote the English ambassador in Paris in 1566: "The Queen's Majesty would fain have a tailor that had skill to make her apparel both after the Italian and French manner; . . . you might . . . obtain some one that serveth the French queen, without mentioning any manner of request in our queen's majesty's name." Cecil was not successful, but Elizabeth's own tailor, Walter Fyshe, solved the problem temporarily by remaking a gown "brought out of Fraunce." He later made a simple linen dress to the queen's measurements and sent it to France as a model for gowns to be made for her there.

After measuring, a tailor cuts a piece of fabric as two assistants tend to their needlework. Finished pieces—including a gown with pleats held in place by rods and a weight—hang from above.

"There is nothing in Englande more constant than the inconstancie of attire."

Young Arabella Stuart holds a doll that probably started out as a tiny mannequin in a French gown, sent to an English noblewoman for approval of its dress style.

A treatise of 1581 on the "various costumes of the gentle world" features these three dress styles favored by French noblewomen. Although the necklines and sleeves differ, all feature long, tapered bodices and full skirts with trains.

Stocking the Queen's Wardrobe

Although Elizabeth loved fine clothes, she wished, whenever possible, to acquire them without incurring personal expense. Her subjects used the longstanding custom of presenting gifts to the monarch on New Year's Day and other special occasions to honor her with elegant items for her wardrobe. Depending on their circumstances, nobles, officials, and members of the clergy made gifts to the queen ranging from pairs of stockings or gloves to exquisitely embroidered sleeves, bodices, and petticoats, entire gowns, and elaborate jewelry.

Great pains were taken to ensure that gifts for the queen were suitable and likely to please. Nobles wrote to the Ladies of the Privy Chamber asking for recommendations on style, color, and motifs for embroidery. Sometimes the donor would simply provide a bolt of fine fabric, embroidery silk, and gold fasteners, and order the queen's tailor to make up a garment to Elizabeth's exact measurements.

Gifts came from other royal courts as well. Mary, Queen of Scots—a fine needlewoman—sent her cousin a skirt of crimson satin embroidered with silver that reportedly greatly pleased Elizabeth. Ivan the Terrible, czar of Russia, sent a mountain of riches for the queen's use, including "4 pieces of Persian cloth of gold and two whole pieces of cloth of silver of curious work," a Turkish carpet, skins of ermine

An embroiderer plies his needle on a piece of fabric stretched taut on a frame. An embroiderer named David Smith performed most of the work on Elizabeth's gowns from the beginning of her reign until his death in 1587.

and white spotted lynx, and four bales of black sable containing 40 skins each.

Elizabeth was often generous in return. She gave jewels to her favorites at court and commissioned her tailor Walter Fyshe to make items for her maids of honor or other ladies of rank. Occasionally she would pass on items of her own clothing; since the queen herself often had her own dresses recut or altered, a gift of royal hand-me-downs was in no way insulting to the recipient. The fortunate lady who received such a present knew the material was of the first quality, very expensive, and likely to be decorated with some of the finest embroidery in the world.

"Her majestie never liked any thinge you gave her so well. . . . if my lord and yow ladyship had geven v hundrd pound. in my opennon yt would not have bene so well taken."

Wearing a most elaborate gown decorated with flower, bird, and sea motifs, a gossamer veil adorned with pearls, and a magnificent array of jewels, Elizabeth exudes royal status and grandeur. The fanciful images on the gown's petticoat may have been embroidered by Bess of Hardwick; she commissioned this portrait of the queen.

Glossary

Accession day: November 17, the day on which Elizabeth became queen, celebrated annually by a national holiday with festivities and a tournament, known as the accession day tilts.

Acts of Supremacy: in 1534, the act that made the reigning monarch, Henry VIII, supreme head of the Church of England, with the authority to reform the church; in 1559, the act that made Queen Elizabeth I supreme governor of the Church of England and abolished papal supremacy.

Ale: a dark, heavy alcoholic beverage made from water, malted barley, and spices, consumed within a week because it spoiled quickly. The common everyday drink of the English people.

Alehouse: a drinking establishment where beer and ale were served.

Algonquian: a family of languages spoken by Native Americans generally living in an area from Canada to the Carolinas and from the Atlantic to the Rocky Mountains; a member of a tribe that spoke one of these languages, including the tribe living on or near Roanoke Island in the 16th century.

Apothecary: one who prescribed, mixed, and dispensed drugs and herbal remedies; the third and least prestigious level of the three-tiered medical profession.

Apprentice: a young person learning a trade or skill.

Apprenticeship: a period of time during which a young person learned a skilled trade or craft from an artisan or craftsman.

Armada: a fleet of armed ships, especially the fleet sent in 1588 by Philip II of Spain against England.

Bard, the: name by which Shakespeare is often called.

Barrister: a lawyer who could plead cases on trial in an English court.

Bastion: a well-fortified position or defensive stronghold.

Bawdyhouse: a house of prostitution.

Bearbaiting: a form of gambling involving the setting of dogs, such as mastiffs, on a chained bear.

Bear pits: the arena in which bearbaiting occurred.

Bedchamber: within the queen's compartments, the area where the queen retired; it was accessible only to her most trusted confidants, her maids of honor, and her other personal attendants and was reached only after first passing through the presence chamber and the privy chamber.

Beer: an alcoholic beverage similar to but lighter than ale, with hops, which acted as a preservative, added to the brew.

Benefit of clergy: the privilege claimed by the medieval church of demanding trial and punishment by an ecclesiastical court, which could not inflict the death penalty. The privilege was gradually extended so that by Tudor times it could be claimed by all who could read.

Bilboes: long iron bars, fastened to the floor or ground, to which fetters were attached to shackle the ankles or feet of prisoners.

Bloodletting: the removal of blood, usually from a vein, a common remedy for fevers and many other ailments.

Bloody Mary: the name Mary Tudor (Mary I, Catholic queen of England from 1553-1558) was called because of the many Protestants she condemned to death for heresy.

Book of Common Prayer: the liturgical book used by the Church of England, authorized for such use in 1549 and revised several times until 1662; that version, with a few minor changes, is used by the Church of England today.

Brazier: a metal container for a fire or for burning coals.

Bride-ales: another name for the bride's postwedding feast at which prodigious amounts of ale were drunk.

Bridewells: workhouses or houses of correction; so-called after London's Palace of Bridewell, which was converted into a workhouse for vagrants but eventually became a prison for the poor.

Catholicism: the faith, doctrine, and practice of the Roman Catholic Church.

Caudle: a warm, soothing beverage made of spiced ale and milk, thickened with breadcrumbs and egg yolks.

Cesspool: a covered hole or pit for receiving sewage or wastes from chamber pots.

Chamber pot: a portable container used as a toilet, typically found in bedrooms.

Chapbooks: small books or pamphlets containing poems, stories, ballads, or religious tracts, carried about for sale by peddlers called chapmen.

Charlatan: in Elizabethan times, a huckster, especially of medicines.

Church-ales: fund-raising events held by churches where beer or ale was sold to raise money for the parish.

Church of England: the national Protestant church in England, formally founded during the Reformation, when Henry VIII and Elizabeth I repudiated the supremacy of the pope's authority in England.

Cistern: a container for catching and holding water, usually at or below ground, but occasionally on or near a roof, where it could serve a building's needs by gravity.

Clink (the): originally a London prison; later, slang for any prison or prison cell.

Close-stool: a small, portable, enclosed wooden stool with a hinged lid which, when lifted, revealed a hole, beneath which was a chamber pot.

Coat of arms: an arrangement of heraldic emblems, usually depicted on a shield, indicating ancestry and distinction; originally worn by knights on a cloak, mantle, or coat over their armor to establish identity in battle; by Elizabethan times, a major status symbol.

Cockfight: a form of gambling involving a fight between two gamecocks whose legs were fitted with metal spurs.

Cock pit: a pit in which cockfights were held.

College of Heralds: also called the College of Arms; the group that verified genealogies and awarded coats of arms to those entitled to bear them.

Compendium: in navigation, an instrument that included a compass, a sundial, a nocturnal, and tables listing latitudes and tides for major European ports.

Compositor: one who sets written material into type; a typesetter.

Conduit: an artificial or natural channel or pipe for conveying water.

Consort: the spouse of a monarch.

Consort songs: the music played by an instrumental ensemble using instruments from the same family, such as the strings.

Constable: an official charged with keeping the peace within a township or parish; the governor of a royal castle.

Constable of the Tower: the governor in charge of the Tower of London.

Consumption: pulmonary tuberculosis.

Copernican view: the theory of Copernicus, heretical at the time, that the earth rotates daily on its axis and, along with the other planets, revolves around the sun; it opposed earlier views that the earth was the center of the universe.

Coronation: the act or ceremony of crowning a king or queen or the sovereign's consort.

Corset: a close-fitting undergarment used to support and shape the waistline, hips, and breasts into the prevailing fashion of the day; a close-fitted, often highly decorative outer garment, especially a laced jacket or bodice.

Cosmography: a general description of the world or the universe; the study of the visible universe, including geography and astronomy, useful in making navigational calculations.

Courtier: one in attendance at a sovereign's court.

Court of Wards and Liveries: the body that oversaw the estates and financial affairs of wards of the Crown, including widows, minor heirs of deceased landowners, and mentally incompetent property holders.

Court tennis: a form of tennis played indoors, differing from modern tennis primarily in the shape of the racket and the design of the court, which included a high wall off which the ball could be played.

Cowslips: in England, the fragrant, yellow-flowered primrose, *Primula veris*, which blooms in early spring; widely cultivated both for its ornamental and medicinal value.

Cozen: to cheat, defraud, or mislead in a petty way; to obtain by deceit.

Cunning woman: a woman who claimed magical powers, such as the ability to find lost objects, foretell the future, heal the sick with charms, or win the goodwill of the queen of the fairies.

Dead reckoning: a method of navigation in which position was determined based on rough calculations of the ship's course and the distance traveled.

Drawn and quartered: a gruesome form of punishment in which the condemned was hung, cut down while still living, disemboweled (or "drawn"), beheaded, and cut into four parts.

Ducats: any of the gold coins once used by several European countries.

Duke: a nobleman of the highest rank after a prince.

Earl: a nobleman of the third rank, below a duke and marquess but above a viscount and baron.

Enclosure: the practice of taking the open or common fields, which were farmed communally, and enclosing them with hedges or ditches for the private use of individuals, usually large landowners, thus ending the grazing and tillage rights of villagers over the land.

Eryngo root (erringo root): the root of any of several plants of the genus *Eryngium*, or sea holly, which was often candied and eaten as a sweetmeat.

Esquire: a man who had obtained a coat of arms, belonged to the English gentry, and ranked directly below a knight; he could hope to be knighted.

Farthingale: an underskirt made of a framework of hoops, usually of wire, whalebone, or wood, worn under a lady's skirt so that the skirt fell in a bell shape from the waist.

Fire ship: a small ship filled with explosives and combustibles, torched and set adrift to ride the current and wind toward enemy ships to destroy them or force them to disperse.

Fishmonger: one who bought and sold fish.

Flotilla: a small fleet of ships.

Football: a rough sport favored by the lower classes and roughly equivalent to modern European football (or American soccer) but with fewer rules.

Forecastle: that part of the upper deck of a ship located toward the bow, or front, of the ship.

Freeholder: any small farmer who owned his land and had the right to use or sell it as he saw fit.

Galleries: in an Elizabethan theater, the covered areas containing seats where the wealthy sat, built around three sides of the open courtyard; in palaces and grand manors, large rooms that served as meeting places and as exhibition halls for displaying paintings and tapestries.

Galliard: a lively European court dance, the simplest form of which consisted of five brisk steps followed by a leap in the air.

Gentleman: generally any man above the rank of yeoman farmer, laborer, or tradesman who could afford to support himself without performing manual labor and could comport himself in a civil manner.

Gentleman usher: a personal servant of gentle birth, serving in a royal or noble household, whose duties varied depending on his position within the household.

Gittern: a medieval wire-strung instrument similar to a guitar.

Glover: one who made gloves.

Goodwife: the mistress of a household; the term was once used as a courtesy title before the surname of a married woman not of noble birth.

Gray's Inn: one of the Inns of Court, the most fashionable of the four, which served more as a finishing school for wellborn youths than as a serious academy of law.

Great Rebuilding: following the War of the Roses, the period between about 1570 and 1640 when the wealthy gentry and nobility built new, gracious manors and palaces designed for comfortable living and show rather than defense.

Groundlings: those spectators who stood on the bare ground in the pit of a theater, in front of the stage.

Guild: an association for organizing, regulating, and restricting trade in a particular product or service.

Harpsichord: a triangular-shaped keyboard instrument resembling a grand piano but with a distinctly different tone.

Heresy: any deviation in opinion or doctrine from that espoused by the established religious authority.

Heretic: one who engages in heresy.

Hogshead: a large cask with a capacity ranging from 63 to 140 gallons.

Hornbooks: early primers consisting of a single sheet of parchment mounted on a wooden tablet and protected by a transparent sheet of animal horn; they typically included the alphabet, numbers, and often, the Lord's Prayer.

Hospital: a charitable institution for the refuge, maintenance, or education of the needy, elderly, ill, or young.

Housekeepers: those who were shareholders in a theater company.

House of Commons: the lower house of Parliament, composed of gentlemen of less-than-noble rank elected by and representatives of their fellow landholders.

House of Lords: the upper house of Parliament, composed of nobles and bishops of the church.

Humanists: those scholars interested in language, literature, politics, and history, who were instrumental in the Renaissance revival of interest in classic Greek and Roman writings, values, and philosophy.

Inns of Court: the four elite legal academies in London that had the exclusive right to license barristers and also provided wellborn youths with a good general education.

Irons: fetters; chains or shackles for the ankles or feet.

Jack of plate: a form of body armor consisting of heavy vests made of mail-lined canvas and reinforced underneath with overlapping plates of iron.

Joust: a contest between two mounted knights using lances; a tilting match, often part of a tournament.

Justice of the peace: a gentlemen appointed by the Crown to administer justice, implement and enforce legislation and royal proclamations, and administer minor legal matters within his jurisdiction.

King's evil: another name for scrofula.

King's Men, the: an acting troupe under the patronage of James I, of which Shakespeare was a member.

Knight: in medieval and Elizabethan days, a mounted gentleman-soldier. A knight was the highest rank below the nobility, one step down from a baron and one step up from an esquire. The title was not hereditary.

Knights of the Garter: an honorary English order of knighthood, the highest British civic and military honor obtainable.

Lance: a thrusting weapon with a long wooden shaft and a sharp, metal head used in jousting.

Litter: an enclosed or curtained couch with shafts extending fore and aft for carrying a passenger.

Liturgy: the prescribed form for the public rites and services of Christian ceremonies.

Low Countries: the region that today consists of Belgium, the Netherlands, and Luxembourg.

Lute: a stringed musical instrument with a large, pear-shaped body and a long neck, usually bent just below the tuning pegs, played by plucking the strings with the fingers and frequently used to accompany singers.

Madrigals: songs for two to four voices, using a secular text and usually following a strict poetic form, sung without accompaniment by a musical instrument.

Magna Carta: The "great charter," also called the royal charter, signed by King John at Runnymede in 1215, upon which the basic rights and civil liberties of English freemen were founded.

Maids of honor: unmarried noblewomen who attended the queen and performed personal services for her within the privy chamber but were not part of the official staff of the privy chamber.

Mail: flexible armor made of small, overlapping metal links, scales, or loops; also called chain mail.

Manchet: a loaf of fine wheat bread, also called white bread, eaten only by the wealthy.

Market hall: a covered public building where the village market was held.

Masque: a lavish dramatic entertainment consisting of a mixture of poetry, music, and dance, in which both professional actors and the ladies and gentlemen of the court participated.

Master: on a merchant ship, the captain of the vessel; in a guild, an artist, craftsman, or performer of great skill, qualified to practice independently without supervision and to teach the trade or craft to apprentices.

Mastiffs: an ancient breed of large, exceptionally strong, smooth-coated dogs used in bearbaiting.

Matins: morning devotions.

May Day: May 1, celebrated by various festivities, including sporting events and dancing.

Maypole: a pole, decorated with streamers, around which dancers would perform on May Day.

Middle Temple: one of the four Inns of Court, considered to be the finest of the four for its curriculum in law.

Militiamen: an armed force of ordinary citizens who met regularly for training, weapons inspection, and drill, called to arms only in emergencies.

Minstrels: traveling entertainers who sang and recited poetry and who, after 1572, were defined as vagrants.

Miracle plays: medieval dramas portraying real or fictitious accounts of the lives, miracles, and martyrdom of saints, originally acted out by medieval monks within their cloisters but by the Tudor era, performed at public festivals.

Moots: at the Inns of Court, hypothetical law cases argued and discussed by law students as exercises.

Morality play: a medieval play using allegorical characters to portray the struggle of the soul to achieve salvation.

Musket: a shoulder gun carried by foot soldiers, used from the late 16th century through the 18th century.

Neck verse: a Bible verse, in Latin, typically the first verse of the 51st psalm, that when read (or recited from memory), qualified a criminal as a member of the clergy and thus exempt from trial in civil courts.

New World: the Western Hemisphere, including North, Central, and South America.

Nobility: that class of persons of high birth and rank, specifically, those bearing the hereditary titles of duke, marquess, earl, viscount, and baron. No man joined the nobility except by birth or by elevation thereto by the monarch.

Nocturnal: a navigational device used to locate the polestar.

Oath of Supremacy: under the Act of Supremacy of 1559, the oath that all officers of the church and state were required to take acknowledging the act and their willingness to obey it; the law was later extended to include graduates of universities and the Inns of Court and schoolmasters.

Open-field system: the farming system under which villages and towns divided the surrounding arable land—usually owned by a wealthy landlord—into three large fields, with the farmers leasing and cultivating strips of land scattered throughout those fields.

Orb: a sphere surmounted by a cross, symbolizing the power and justice of the monarch.

Page: a boy trained as a knight's attendant; a youth, usually of noble birth, in ceremonial employment or attendance at court.

Papal bull: a letter or official document from the pope, sealed with a round leaden seal called a bulla.

Parliament: the national legislative body of England, consisting of the House of Lords and the House of Commons and convened only when called by the queen.

Passport: a document permitting free and unmolested travel; a safe-conduct pass that many poor travelers were required to carry under the Poor Laws, stating their destination and the reason for their journey.

Patent: a grant of public land made by a government or monarch conveying to a person fee-simple title to the land in question, or the land so granted.

Patron: a benefactor; one who financially and morally encouraged and supported an artist, such as a poet or musician, in his work.

Peer of the realm: a male member of the nobility; that is, a duke, marquess, earl, viscount, or baron, with the right to a seat in the House of Lords.

Pensioners: gentlemen-at-arms who attended a monarch.

Petticoat: an outer skirt or richly decorated and embroidered underskirt worn with an outerskirt specifically designed to reveal the lavish petticoat beneath; an underskirt worn for warmth or, when several were worn together, to create volume in place of a farthingale.

Physicians: the most prestigious level of the three-tiered medical profession; although university trained, physicians had limited healing skills, and their knowledge was primarily theoretical; their contact with patients was commonly limited to a wealthy few.

Pike: a weapon of war consisting of a long wooden shaft with a pointed steel head, used by foot soldiers.

Pillory: a wooden device consisting of a framework with holes for the head and hands in which offenders were locked for public ridicule.

Pilot: one who steers a ship, either permanently, as the helmsman on an oceangoing vessel, or temporarily, as the person who conducts the ship into and out of port or through certain dangerous waters.

Piracy: the act of using an armed ship to appropriate property (usually another ship and its contents) belonging to someone else.

Plague: any acute, highly contagious, and usually fatal bacterial disease, particularly bubonic or pneumonic plague.

Plead their bellies: to claim to be pregnant; a plea women would make to temporarily avoid execution.

Plough Monday: the first day of the plowing season in late winter and the beginning of the agricultural year.

Polestar: the North Star, called Polaris, located at the tip of the tail of the Little Dipper or Great Bear (Ursa Minor) in the northern constellation. A point useful in making navigational calculations.

Pomanders: a mixture of aromatic herbs and spices enclosed in a bag or perforated container and held to the nose to mask unpleasant odors.

Poor Laws: a body of legislation enacted over a number of years, but primarily during the reign of Elizabeth I, that imposed taxes upon the population for the relief of the deserving poor and that attempted to distinguish between

these souls and the underserving poor, in an effort to help the former and punish the latter.

Presence chamber: within the queen's compartments, those rooms used for public ceremonies and in which the queen received visitors.

Pressman: a printing press operator, covering pages of type with ink and preparing the paper for printing.

Primero: a card game, the object being to acquire certain combinations of cards, with specific scoring values. An early forerunner of modern poker.

Privateer: an armed, privately owned ship authorized by a government during wartime to prey upon and capture or sink the war- or merchant ships of the enemy; the commander of such a ship.

Privie (privy): a very small room set in an outside wall, with a seat placed over a shaft that drained into a pit below; an outhouse or outdoor toilet.

Privy chamber: the monarch's private chamber at court where he or she retired for private affairs and meetings of a confidential nature.

Privy Council: those men appointed to advise Elizabeth I and to administer England's affairs.

Progress: an official and ceremonial journey, made periodically through a monarch's realm, during which the monarch was housed by the nobility along the way and elaborate celebrations were held en route for the monarch's entertainment.

Protégé: one whose welfare, training, or career is under the protection and guidance of another.

Puritanism: the austere faith, doctrine, and practice of the Puritans, characterized by a stern morality and hostility to frivolity, social pleasures, or personal indulgences.

Puritans: English Protestants who espoused a stern religious philosophy and the simplification of religious practices during the 16th and 17th centuries.

Purveyor: one who furnishes provisions, especially food, to an establishment. In the case of the queen's household, one who had the right to purchase supplies at fixed prices.

Quacksalver: a quack; one who pretends to have medical knowledge and skill.

Quay: a wharf or reinforced bank for loading and unloading ships and barges.

Rack: an instrument of torture consisting of a large frame with rollers at either end to which the limbs were fastened and between which the body was stretched.

Rapier: a long, slender, two-edged sword used for thrusting.

Receipt book: a book filled with recipes for foods, home remedies, and household formulas and hints.

Recusant: a Roman Catholic who refused to acknowledge the authority of the Church of England and to attend services, thus incurring fines and other penalties.

Reformation: a religious movement in western Europe, beginning in the early 16th century and intended to reform some doctrines and practices of the Roman Catholic Church; it ultimately led to the rejection of Roman authority and the establishment of Protestant churches throughout Europe, including the Church of England.

Regrater: one who would buy foodstuffs in one market and resell them for a profit in or within four miles of that market; a wholesaler or middleman.

Riding skimmington: a ritual wherein a henpecked hus-

band (the skimmington), or someone impersonating him, was paraded through the streets atop a pole, usually amid a clamor of bells and general commotion. Also known as riding the stang.

Rigging: the system of ropes, chains, etc. that support or raise and lower the masts, sails, and spars of a ship.

Scrofula: a form of tuberculosis characterized by the enlargement and degeneration of the lymph nodes, mainly of the neck. Also called the king's evil, because it was believed that it could be cured by the touch of a monarch.

Scurvy: a disease caused by a deficiency of vitamin C, characterized by bleeding gums, excessive bruising, sore, stiff joints, and extreme weakness; a major cause of disability and death among sailors until 1753, when its cause, prevention, and cure were determined.

Sea dogs: experienced sailors.

Scepter: a staff carried by a sovereign as an emblem of authority.

Shipwright: one who draws up plans for, builds, and repairs ships.

Shrovetide: the three days before Ash Wednesday, the beginning of the 40 days of Lent.

Simples: medicinal plants; herbal remedies made at home from such plants.

Sixpence: a coin worth six pennies.

Skeffington's gyves: an instrument of torture that compressed a person's body into a broken ball.

Sons of Ben: playwrights who were protégés of Ben Jonson.

Sounding leads: the metal weight at the end of a sounding line, a line marked at intervals of fathoms, used to measure the depth of water.

Starboard: that side of a ship on the right hand of a person standing on the ship and facing the ship's bow.

Sundial: a timekeeping device showing the time of day by the position of a shadow on a style.

Surcoat: a tunic or tuniclike cloak worn by a knight over his armor.

Surgeons: the second level of the three-tiered medical profession, men whose knowledge and skills were based, not on theory, but by practice in treating wounds of various sorts, frequently on the battlefield.

Sweetmeats: any sweet treat, particularly candies and candied fruit.

Sword: a weapon with a long, straight (or slightly curved) sharp-pointed blade with either one or two cutting edges, set into a hilt.

Tapestries: heavy wool or silk handwoven textiles, with rich, multicolored designs or scenes built up as the piece was woven, often occurring in sets of six or more panels, used as decorative wall hangings in galleries.

Tilt yard: an enclosed yard for jousting.

Timber and thatch: a building construction method using half-timber framing usually filled in with plaster or brick; it had a steep, thatched roof.

Tinkers: itinerant menders of metal household goods, such as pans; after 1572, classified as vagrants.

Tournament: a pageant with elaborate codes of conduct; it included jousting, tilting, and various other contests.

Tower of London: also called the Tower. Built originally by William the Conqueror as a fortress in the 11th century and continually expanded until, by the mid-16th century, it was an 18-acre complex with at least 19 towers, surrounded by a water-filled moat 100 feet across and by several walls.

Vagrants: vagabonds, tramps. Individuals with no regular means of support and usually no permanent home, seen as a threat to social order and the community.

Venery: sexual intercourse or the pursuit thereof.

Viol: a musical instrument that looked like, but was larger than, the violin, with a deeper tone.

Virginal: a small keyboard instrument similar to a harpsichord but rectangular in shape and with no legs.

Virgin Queen: the name by which Queen Elizabeth was often called.

Wake: a vigil over a dead body before burial, accompanied in Elizabethan times by singing, games, and drunken merriment; an annual parish festival held in commemoration of the dedication of a church or in honor of the church's patron saint.

Warder: a prison guard; jailer.

War of the Roses: a series of wars occurring from 1455 to 1485 between the Houses of Lancaster and York for possession of the English throne.

Water closet: a room containing a toilet similar to a close-stool.

Wherry: a small, upholstered, oar-propelled boat used for both travel and commerce on the Thames River.

White meats: not meat at all, but the eggs, butter, milk, curds, cream, whey, and cheese upon which the lower class subsisted, along with brown bread.

Wise women: Elizabethan healers who typically treated other women; often equated with witches by Elizabethans.

Wizards: those who practiced magic; sorcerers; after 1572, defined as vagrants.

Yardarm: either end of the long tapering spar slung to a mast to support and spread the head of a square sail.

Yeoman: a freeman who owned and farmed his own land and was in a social class above that of a laborer but below that of the gentry; an attendant, retainer, guard, or other subordinate official in a noble or royal household.

Acknowledgments & Picture Credits

ACKNOWLEDGMENTS

The editors wish to thank the following individuals and institutions for their assistance in the preparation of this volume:
Philip Abbott, Royal Armouries, Leeds, Yorkshire; Jean Archibald, Edinburgh University Library, Edinburgh; John Freeman, West Wickham, Kent; Robin Harcourt-Williams, Hatfield House, Hatfield, Hertfordshire; Dr. Kate Harris, Longleat House, Warminster, Wiltshire; Theresa M. Helein, Folger Shakespeare Library, Washington, D.C.; Mary Ison and staff, Library of Congress, Washington, D.C.; Jean Miller, Folger Shakespeare Library, Washington, D.C.; Capt. Dermot Rhodes, Lord Leycester Hospital, Warwick, Warwickshire; Mike Spain, The Honourable Society of the Middle Temple, London; Edward Tilley, Public Record Office, Kew, Surrey; Laetitia Yeandle, Folger Shakespeare Library, Washington, D.C.; Robert Yorke, The College of Arms, London; Reading Room staff of the Folger Shakespeare Library, Washington, D.C.

Bibliography

BOOKS

Abraham, Gerald, ed. and comp. *The Age of Humanism, 1540-1630.* London: Oxford University Press, 1968.

Adamson, J. H., and H. F. Folland. *The Shepherd of the Ocean.* Boston: Gambit, 1969.

Alley, Hugh. *Hugh Alley's Caveat.* Ed. by Ian Archer, Caroline Barron, and Vanessa Harding. London: London Topographical Society, 1988.

Andrews, Kenneth R.:
   "Elizabethan Privateering." In *Raleigh in Exeter, 1985.* Ed. by Joyce Youings. Exeter, U.K.: University of Exeter, 1985.
   Trade, Plunder, and Settlement. Cambridge: Cambridge University Press, 1984.

Archer, Ian W. *The Pursuit of Stability.* Cambridge: Cambridge University Press, 1991.

Arnold, Janet, ed. *Queen Elizabeth's Wardrobe Unlock'd.* Leeds, U.K.: Maney, 1988.

Beier, A. L. *Masterless Men.* London: Methuen, 1985.

Beier, Lucinda McCray. *Sufferers and Healers.* London: Routledge & Kegan Paul, 1987.

Bell, H. E. *An Introduction to the History and Records of the Court of Wards and Liveries.* Cambridge: Cambridge University Press, 1953.

Bennett, H. S. *English Books and Readers, 1558 to 1603.* Cambridge: Cambridge University Press, 1965.

Blackstone, G. V. *A History of the British Fire Service.* London: Routledge & Kegan Paul, 1957.

Blayney, Peter W. M. *The Bookshops in Paul's Cross Churchyard.* London: Bibliographical Society, 1990.

Boynton, Lindsay. *The Elizabethan Militia, 1558-1638.* London: Routledge & Kegan Paul, 1967.

Bridenbaugh, Carl. *Vexed and Troubled Englishmen, 1590-1642.* New York: Oxford University Press, 1968.

Brooke, Iris. *English Costume in the Age of Elizabeth.* New York: Barnes & Noble, 1950.

Byrne, M. St. Clare. *Elizabethan Life in Town and Country.* London: University Paperbacks (Methuen), 1961.

Caldwell, John. *The Oxford History of English Music, Volume 1: From the Beginnings to c.1715.* Oxford: Clarendon Press, 1991.

Cannon, John, and Ralph Griffiths. *The Oxford Illustrated History of the British Monarchy.* Oxford: Oxford University Press, 1988.

Capp, Bernard. *English Almanacs, 1500-1800.* Ithaca, N.Y.: Cornell University Press, 1979.

Chambers, E. K. *The Elizabethan Stage* (Vol. 2). Oxford: Clarendon Press, 1923.

Charlton, John, ed. *The Tower of London.* London: H.M.S.O., 1978.

Chute, Marchette. *Shakespeare of London.* New York: Book-of-the-Month Club, 1996.

Clair, Colin. *Kitchen and Table.* London: Abelard-Schuman, 1965.

Clark, Peter. *The English Alehouse.* London: Longman, 1983.

Clark, Sandra. *The Elizabethan Pamphleteers.* London: Athlone Press, 1983.

Cook, Judith. *The Golden Age of the English Theatre.* London: Simon & Schuster, 1995.

Corbett, Julian S., ed. *Papers Relating to the Navy during the Spanish War: 1585-1587.* Brookfield, Vt.: Temple Smith, 1987.

Craig, D. H. *Sir John Harington.* Boston: Twayne Publishers, 1985.

Crawford, Patricia. *Women and Religion in England, 1500-1720.* London: Routledge, 1993.

Cumming, Valerie. *Royal Dress.* London: B. T. Batsford, 1989.

Cummins, John. *Francis Drake.* New York: St. Martin's Press, 1995.

Cunnington, Phillis, and Catherine Lucas. *Charity Costumes of Children, Scholars, Almsfolk, Pensioners.* London: Adam & Charles Black, 1978.

Davis, Michael Justin. *The England of William Shakespeare.* New York: E. P. Dutton, 1987.

Davis, William Stearns. *Life in Elizabethan Days.* New York: Harper & Brothers, 1930.

Doran, Susan. *Elizabeth I and Religion, 1558-1603.* London: Routledge, 1994.

Doran, Susan, and Christopher Durston. *Princes, Pastors, and People.* London: Routledge, 1991.

Dovey, Zillah. *An Elizabethan Progress.* Madison, N.J.: Fairleigh Dickinson University Press, 1996.

Dunlop, Ian. *Palaces and Progresses of Elizabeth I.* New York: Taplinger, 1970.

Elton, G. R. *The Parliament of England, 1559-1581.* Cambridge: Cambridge University Press, 1986.

English Plans for North America (Vol. 3 of New American World). Ed. by David B. Quinn. New York: Arno Press, 1979.

Erickson, Carolly. *The First Elizabeth.* New York: Summit Books, 1983.

Feltwell, John. *The Story of Silk.* New York: St. Martin's Press, 1990.

Feuerlicht, Roberta Strauss. *The Life and World of Henry VIII.* New York: Crowell-Collier Press, 1970.

Fletcher, Anthony. *Gender, Sex, and Subordination in England, 1500-1800.* New Haven, Conn.: Yale University Press, 1995.

Fraser, Antonia. *Mary Queen of Scots.* New York: Delacorte Press, 1969.

French, Peter J. *John Dee.* London: Routledge & Kegan Paul, 1972.

Frye, Susan. *Elizabeth I.* New York: Oxford University Press, 1993.

Gerard, John. *John Gerard.* Trans. by Philip Caraman. London: Longmans, Green, 1951.

Girouard, Mark:
   Hardwick Hall. London: The National Trust, 1996.
   Robert Smythson and the Elizabethan Country House. New Haven, Conn.: Yale University Press, 1983.

Glanville, Philippa. *Silver in Tudor and Early Stuart England.* London: Victoria and Albert Museum, 1990.

Great Britain Historical Manuscripts Commission. *Calendar of the Manuscripts of the Most Hon. the Marquis of Salisbury, K.G.* London: H.M.S.O., 1894.

Green, Mary Anne Everett, ed. *Calendar of State Papers: Domestic Series, of the Reign of Elizabeth, 1591-1594.* London: Longmans, Green, Reader, and Dyer, 1867.

Griffiths, Paul. *Youth and Authority.* Oxford: Clarendon Press, 1996.

Hackett, Helen. *Virgin Mother, Maiden Queen.* New York: St. Martin's Press, 1995.

Haigh, Christopher. *Elizabeth I.* London: Longman, 1988.

Hale, John R., and the Editors of Time-Life Books. *Age of Exploration* (Great Ages of Man series). Amsterdam: Time-Life Books, 1966.

Haller, William. *Foxe's Book of Martyrs and the Elect Nation.* London: Jonathan Cape, 1963.

Harington, John. *Nugae Antiquae* (Vol. 2). Ed. by Henry Harington. Hildesheim, Germany: Georg Olms Verlagsbuchhandlung, 1968 (reprint of 1779 edition).

Harris, Tim, ed. *Popular Culture in England, c.1500-1850.* New York: St. Martin's Press, 1995.

Harrison, G. B.:
  Elizabethan Plays and Players. London: George Routledge and Sons, 1940.
  The Life and Death of Robert Devereux, Earl of Essex. New York: Henry Holt, 1937.
  The Story of Elizabethan Drama. New York: Octagon Books (Farrar, Straus and Giroux), 1973.

Harrison, William. *The Description of England.* Ed. by Georges Edelen. Washington, D.C.: Folger Shakespeare Library, 1994.

Hart, Roger. *English Life in Tudor Times.* London: Wayland, 1972.

Haynes, Alan. *Invisible Power.* New York: St. Martin's Press, 1992.

Hearn, Karen, ed. *Dynasties: Painting in Tudor and Jacobean England, 1530-1630.* New York: Rizzoli, 1996.

Herford, C. H., and Percy Simpson, eds. *Ben Jonson* (Vol. 1). Oxford: Clarendon Press, 1925.

Hibbert, Christopher. *The Virgin Queen.* Reading, Mass.: Addison-Wesley, 1991.

Hind, Arthur M.:
  Engraving in England in the Sixteenth and Seventeenth Centuries:
  The Tudor Period (Part 1). Cambridge: Cambridge University Press, 1952.
  The Reign of James I (Part 2). Cambridge: Cambridge University Press, 1955.

Historical Dictionary of Tudor England, 1485-1603. New York: Greenwood Press, 1991.

Holmes, Martin. *Elizabethan London.* London: Cassell, 1969.

Hurstfield, Joel. *The Queen's Wards.* London: Longmans, Green, 1958.

Hurstfield, Joel, and Alan G. R. Smith, eds. *Elizabethan People: State and Society.* New York: St. Martin's Press, 1972.

Hutton, Ronald. *The Rise and Fall of Merry England.* Oxford: Oxford University Press, 1994.

James, Mervyn. *Society, Politics, and Culture.* Cambridge: Cambridge University Press, 1986.

Johnson, Paul. *Elizabeth I.* London: Weidenfeld and Nicolson, 1974.

Jones, Norman. *The Birth of the Elizabethan Age.* Oxford: Blackwell, 1993.

Joseph, B. L. *Shakespeare's Eden.* London: Blandford Press, 1971.

Keeler, Mary Frear, ed. *Sir Francis Drake's West Indian Voyage, 1585-86.* London: Hakluyt Society, 1981.

Kemp, Peter. *The British Sailor.* London: J M Dent & Sons, 1970.

Kraus, Hans P. *Sir Francis Drake.* Amsterdam: N. Israel, 1970.

Lace, William W. *Elizabethan England.* San Diego, Calif.: Lucent Books, 1995.

Lacey, Robert. *Robert, Earl of Essex.* London: Weidenfeld and Nicolson, 1971.

Leonard, E. M. *The Early History of English Poor Relief.* Cambridge: Cambridge University Press, 1900.

Levin, Carole. *"The Heart and Stomach of a King."* Philadelphia: University of Pennsylvania Press, 1994.

Levine, Joseph M., ed. *Elizabeth I.* Englewood Cliffs, N.J.: Prentice-Hall, 1969.

Loades, David:
  The Tudor Court. Gwynedd, U.K.: Headstart History, 1992.
  The Tudor Navy. Aldershot, Hants, U.K.: Scolar Press, 1992.

London before the Fire. London: Sidgwick & Jackson, 1973.

London in the Age of Shakespeare. Ed. by Lawrence Manley. University Park: Pennsylvania State University Press, 1986.

Low, Anthony. *Augustine Baker.* New York: Twayne, 1970.

MacCaffrey, Wallace T.:
  Elizabeth I. London: Edward Arnold, 1993.
  Elizabeth I: War and Politics, 1588-1603. Princeton, N.J.: Princeton University Press, 1992.
  Queen Elizabeth and the Making of Policy, 1572-1588. Princeton, N.J.: Princeton University Press, 1981.
  The Shaping of the Elizabethan Regime. Princeton, N.J.: Princeton University Press, 1968.

McCann, Justin, and Hugh Connolly, eds. *Memorials of Father Augustine Baker and Other Documents Relating to the English Benedictines.* London: Catholic Record Society, 1933.

McGrath, Patrick. *Papists and Puritans under Elizabeth I.* London: Blandford Press, 1967.

McLean, Antonia. *Humanism and the Rise of Science in Tudor England.* New York: Neale Watson Academic Publications, 1972.

Madox, Richard. *An Elizabethan in 1582.* Ed. by Elizabeth Story Donno. London: Hakluyt Society, 1976.

Manningham, John. *The Diary of John Manningham of the Middle Temple, 1602-1603.* Ed. by Robert Parker Sorlein. Hanover, N.H.: University Press of New England, 1976.

Manzione, Carol Kazmierczak. *Christ's Hospital of London, 1552-1598.* London: Associated University Presses, 1995.

Markham, Gervase. *The English Housewife.* Kingston, Quebec: McGill-Queen's University Press, 1986.

Marrin, Albert. *The Sea King.* New York: Atheneum (Simon & Schuster), 1995.

Marshall, Rosalind K.:
  Elizabeth I. London: H.M.S.O., 1991.
  Queen of Scots. Edinburgh: H.M.S.O., 1986.

Marshburn, Joseph H. *Murder and Witchcraft in England, 1550-1640.* Norman: University of Oklahoma Press, 1971.

Martin, Colin, and Geoffrey Parker. *The Spanish Armada.* New York: W. W. Norton, 1988.

Mason, Anita. *An Illustrated Dictionary of Jewellery.* New York: Harper & Row, 1974.

Mathews, Nieves. *Francis Bacon.* New Haven, Conn.: Yale University Press, 1996.

Mattingly, Garrett. *The Armada.* Boston: Houghton Mifflin, 1959.

May, Steven W. *Sir Walter Ralegh.* Boston: Twayne, 1989.

Meyer, Carl S. *Elizabeth I and the Religious Settlement of 1559.* St. Louis: Concordia, 1960.

Miles, Rosalind. *Ben Jonson.* London: Routledge & Kegan Paul, 1986.

Miller, Edwin Haviland. *The Professional Writer in Elizabethan England.* Cambridge, Mass.: Harvard University Press, 1959.

Miller, Jean, Francie Owens, and Rachel Doggett. *The Housewife's Rich Cabinet.* Washington, D.C.: Folger Shakespeare Library, 1997.

Mowl, Timothy. *Elizabethan and Jacobean Style.* London: Phaidon Press, 1993.

Neale, J. E.:
  Elizabeth I and Her Parliaments, 1559-1581. London: Jonathan Cape, 1953.
  Queen Elizabeth I. London: Jonathan Cape, 1934.

New Catholic Encyclopedia (Vol. 6). Washington, D.C.: Catholic University of America, 1967.

Nicoll, Allardyce, ed.:
  The Elizabethans. Cambridge: Cambridge University Press, 1957.
  Shakespeare in His Own Age. Cambridge: Cambridge University Press, 1964.

Orlin, Lena Cowen. *Elizabethan Households.* Washington, D.C.: Folger Shakespeare Library, 1995.

The Oxford Encyclopedia of the Reformation (Vol. 3). New York: Oxford University Press, 1996.

The Oxford Illustrated History of Britain. Ed. by Kenneth O. Morgan. Oxford: Oxford University Press, 1984.

The Oxford Illustrated History of Tudor and Stuart Britain. Ed. by John Morrill. Oxford: Oxford University Press, 1996.

Palliser, Bury, Mrs. *History of Lace.* Ed. by M. Jourdain and Alice Dryden. New York: Dover, 1984.

Palliser, D. M. *The Age of Elizabeth.* London: Longman, 1983.

Parker, Michael St. John. "William Shakespeare." In *William Shakespeare: Stratford-upon-Avon and Southwark.* Ed. by Jane Drake. Andover, Hants, U.K.: Pitkin, 1990.

Partridge, John. *The Treasurie of Hidden Secrets.* London: n.p., 1627.

Pearson, Lu Emily. *Elizabethans at Home.* Stanford, Calif.: Stanford University Press, 1957.

Perry, Maria. *The Word of a Prince.* Rochester, N.Y.: Boydell Press, 1990.

Plat, Hugh. *Delightes for Ladies.* London: Crosby Lockwood & Son, 1948.

Platter, Thomas. *Thomas Platter's Travels in England, 1599.* Trans. by Clare Williams. London: Jonathan Cape, 1937.

Pomeroy, Elizabeth W. *Reading the Portraits of Queen Eliza-*

beth I. Hamden, Conn.: Archon Books, 1989.

Pound, John:

Poverty and Vagrancy in Tudor England. Harlow, Essex, U.K.: Longman, 1971.

Tudor and Stuart Norwich. Chichester, Sussex, U.K.: Phillimore, 1988.

Prest, Wilfrid R.:

The Inns of Court under Elizabeth I and the Early Stuarts, 1590-1640. London: Longman, 1972.

The Rise of the Barristers. Oxford: Clarendon Press, 1986.

Prockter, Adrian, and Robert Taylor, comps. The A to Z of Elizabethan London. London: London Topographical Society, 1979.

Quinn, David Beers. Set Fair for Roanoke. Chapel Hill: University of North Carolina Press, 1985.

Read, Conyers:

Mr. Secretary Cecil and Queen Elizabeth. London: Jonathan Cape, 1955.

Mr. Secretary Walsingham and the Policy of Queen Elizabeth (Vol. 2). Hamden, Conn.: Archon Books, 1967.

Reed, Michael. The Age of Exuberance, 1550-1700. London: Routledge & Kegan Paul, 1986.

Regan, Geoffrey. Elizabethan England. London: B. T. Batsford, 1990.

The Reign of Elizabeth I: Court and Culture in the Last Decade. Ed. by John Guy. Cambridge: Cambridge University Press, 1995.

Ridley, Jasper. The Tudor Age. London: Constable, 1988.

Riggs, David. Ben Jonson. Cambridge, Mass.: Harvard University Press, 1989.

Rivals in Power. Ed. by David Starkey. New York: Grove Weidenfeld, 1990.

The Roanoke Voyages, 1584-1590 (Vol. 1). Ed. by David Beers Quinn. New York: Dover Publications, 1991.

Rodríguez-Salgado, M. J., and the Staff of the National Maritime Museum. Armada, 1588-1988. London: Penguin Books, 1988.

Rowse, A. L.:

The Elizabethan Renaissance. New York: Charles Scribner's Sons, 1972.

The England of Elizabeth. Madison: University of Wisconsin Press, 1978.

Saint, Andrew, and Gillian Darley. The Chronicles of London. New York: St. Martin's Press, 1994.

Salgādo, Gāmini. The Elizabethan Underworld. New York: St. Martin's Press, 1992.

Sass, Lorna J. To the Queen's Taste. New York: Metropolitan Museum of Art, 1976.

Scarisbrick, Diana:

Jewellery in Britain, 1066-1837. Wilby, Norwich, U.K.: Michael Russell, 1994.

Tudor and Jacobean Jewellery. London: Tate Publishing, 1995.

Schoenbaum, S. Shakespeare. Oxford: Oxford University Press, 1979.

Schofield, John. The Building of London. London: British Museum Publications, 1984.

Schofield, John, ed. The London Surveys of Ralph Treswell. London: London Topographical Society, 1987.

Shakespeare's England (Vols. 1 and 2). Oxford: Clarendon

Press, 1917.

Sharp, Thomas. A Dissertation on the Pageants or Dramatic Mysteries. Coventry, U.K.: Merhidew and Son, 1925.

Shirley, John W.:

Sir Walter Ralegh and the New World. Raleigh: North Carolina Department of Cultural Resources, 1985.

Thomas Harriot. Oxford: Clarendon Press, 1983.

Simon, Edith, and the Editors of Time-Life Books. The Reformation (Great Ages of Man series). New York: Time-Life Books, 1966.

Slack, Paul:

The English Poor Law, 1531-1782. Cambridge: Cambridge University Press, 1990.

Poverty and Policy in Tudor and Stuart England. London: Longman, 1988.

Smith, Lacey Baldwin. The Horizon Book of the Elizabethan World. New York: American Heritage, 1967.

Somerset, Anne. Elizabeth I. New York: Alfred A. Knopf, 1991.

Sommerville, C. John. The Secularization of Early Modern England. New York: Oxford University Press, 1992.

Spurling, Hilary. Elinor Fettiplace's Receipt Book. New York: Viking Penguin, 1986.

Strong, Roy:

The Cult of Elizabeth. Berkeley: University of California Press, 1977.

The English Renaissance Miniature. New York: Thames and Hudson, 1983.

The Story of Britain. New York: Fromm International, 1996.

Stuart England. Ed. by Blair Worden. Oxford: Phaidon, 1986.

Sugden, John. Sir Francis Drake. New York: Henry Holt, 1990.

Taylor, E. G. R., ed. The Troublesome Voyage of Captain Edward Fenton, 1582-1583. Cambridge: Cambridge University Press, 1959.

Torture and Punishment. London: H.M.S.O., 1975.

Viles, Edward, and F. J. Furnivall, eds. The Rogues and Vagabonds of Shakespeare's Youth. New York: Duffield, 1907.

Walker, Bryce, and the Editors of Time-Life Books. The Armada (The Seafarers series). Alexandria, Va.: Time-Life Books, 1981.

Watt, Tessa. Cheap Print and Popular Piety, 1550-1640. Cambridge: Cambridge University Press, 1991.

Weinstein, Rosemary. Tudor London. London: H.M.S.O., 1994.

Weir, Alison:

The Children of Henry VIII. New York: Ballantine Books, 1996.

The Six Wives of Henry VIII. New York: Ballantine Books, 1991.

White, Helen C. Social Criticism in Popular Religious Literature of the Sixteenth Century. New York: Octagon Books (Farrar, Straus and Giroux), 1973.

Whythorne, Thomas. The Autobiography of Thomas Whythorne. Ed. by James M. Osborn. Oxford: Clarendon Press, 1961.

William Shakespeare: The Complete Works. New York: Gramercy Books, 1975.

Williams, George Walton. The Craft of Printing and the Publication of Shakespeare's Works. Washington: Folger Books, 1985.

Williams, Neville:

All the Queen's Men. New York: Macmillan, 1972.

The Life and Times of Elizabeth I. Garden City, N.Y.: Doubleday, 1972.

Thomas Howard, Fourth Duke of Norfolk. New York: E. P. Dutton, 1964.

Williams, Penry:

The Later Tudors. Oxford: Clarendon Press, 1995.

Life in Tudor England. London: B. T. Batsford, 1964.

Wilson, C. Anne. Food and Drink in Britain. London: Constable, 1973.

Wilson, Derek:

Sweet Robin. London: Hamish Hamilton, 1981.

The Tower of London. New York: Barnes & Noble, 1978.

Wilson, Jean. The Archaeology of Shakespeare. Stroud, Gloucestershire, U.K.: Alan Sutton, 1995.

Witchcraft in England, 1558-1618. Ed. by Barbara Rosen. Amherst: University of Massachusetts Press, 1991.

Wolf, A. A History of Science, Technology, and Philosophy in the 16th and 17th Centuries (Vol. 1). New York: Harper & Brothers, 1959.

Wright, Louis B. Middle-Class Culture in Elizabethan England. Ithaca, N.Y.: Cornell University Press, 1958.

Youings, Joyce. Sixteenth-Century England. London: Allen Lane, 1984.

PERIODICALS

Barron, Caroline, Christopher Coleman, and Claire Gobbi, eds. "The London Journal of Alessandro Magno, 1562." London Journal, 1982, Vol. 9, no. 2.

Bovill, E. W. "The 'Madre de Dios.' " Mariner's Mirror, 1968, Vol. 54.

"Hardwick Hall: 400 Years." National Trust Magazine, Spring 1997.

Ingram, Martin. "Ridings, Rough Music, and the 'Reform of Popular Culture' in Early Modern England." Past & Present, November 1984.

Reid, R. R. "The Rebellion of the Earls, 1569." Transactions of the Royal Historical Society, 1905, Vol. 20.

A Review of the History of the North of England and the Borders. Entire issue of Northern History, 1992, Vol. 28.

Wescher, H. "Fashions and Textiles of Queen Elizabeth's Reign." Ciba Review, February 1950.

OTHER SOURCES

Baumfylde, Mary. "Medical and Cookery Recipes, June 1626." Microfilm. Washington, D.C.: Folger Shakespeare Library, n.d.

Harris, John, Stephen Orgel, and Roy Strong. "The King's Arcadia: Inigo Jones and the Stuart Court." Show catalog. Banqueting House, Whitehall, London, July 12-September 2, 1973.

Strong, Roy. "Festival Designs by Inigo Jones." Show catalog. International Exhibitions Foundation, 1967-1968.

Vanes, Jean. "Education and Apprenticeship in Sixteenth-Century Bristol." Lecture delivered at the University of Bristol, May 1981. Available from the Bristol branch of The Historical Association, University of Bristol.

Index

Time-Life Books is a division of Time Life Inc.

TIME LIFE INC.
PRESIDENT and CEO: George Artandi

TIME-LIFE BOOKS
PRESIDENT: Stephen R. Frary
PUBLISHER/MANAGING EDITOR: Neil Kagan

What Life Was Like ®
IN THE REALM OF ELIZABETH

EDITOR: Denise Dersin
DIRECTOR, NEW PRODUCT DEVELOPMENT:
Elizabeth D. Ward
DIRECTORS OF MARKETING:
Pamela R. Farrell, Joseph A. Kuna

Deputy Editor: Marion Ferguson Briggs
Art Director: Alan Pitts
Text Editor: Stephen G. Hyslop
Associate Editors/Research and Writing:
Jarelle S. Stein, Sharon Kurtz Thompson
Senior Copyeditor: Mary Beth Oelkers-Keegan
Technical Art Specialist: John Drummond
Picture Coordinator: David Herod
Editorial Assistant: Christine Higgins

Special Contributors: Charlotte Anker, Ronald H. Bailey,
Ellen Phillips (chapter text); Mark Galan, Diane Gerard,
Christine Hauser, Stacy W. Hoffhaus, Marilyn Murphy
Terrell, Elizabeth Thompson, Myrna Traylor-Herndon
(research-writing); Beth Levin (research); Janet Cave (edit-
ing); Ann Lee Bruen (copyediting); Lina Baber Burton
(glossary); Barbara L. Klein (index and overread).

Correspondents: Christine Hinze (London), Christina
Lieberman (New York) Maria Vincenza Aloisi (Paris).
Valuable assistance was also provided by:
Angelika Lemmer (Bonn).

Director of Finance: Christopher Hearing
Directors of Book Production: Marjann Caldwell,
Patricia Pascale
Director of Publishing Technology: Betsi McGrath
Director of Photography and Research: John Conrad Weiser
Director of Editorial Administration: Barbara Levitt
Production Manager: Gertraude Schaefer
Quality Assurance Manager: James King
Chief Librarian: Louise D. Forstall

Consultant:
Norman Jones is professor of history and chair of the
department of history at Utah State University. He is the
author of many books and articles on Elizabethan England, including *The Birth of the Elizabethan Age: England in
the 1560s; God and the Moneylenders: Usury and Law in Early Modern England;* and *Faith by Statute: Parliament and the
Settlement of Religion, 1559.* He also coedited *The Parliaments of Elizabethan England.* A graduate of Cambridge
University, Dr. Jones is a Fellow of the Royal Historical
Society of Great Britain.

Library of Congress Cataloging-in-Publication Data
What life was like in the realm of Elizabeth :
England, AD 1533-1603 /
by the editors of Time-Life Books.
     p.   cm.
     Includes bibliographical references and index.
     ISBN 0-7835-5456-7
     1. England—Social life and customs—16th century.
2. Great Britain—History—Elizabeth, 1558-1603.
I. Time-Life Books.
DA320.5W48 1998   98-13020
942.05'5—dc21   CIP

Other Publications:
HISTORY
The American Story
Voices of the Civil War
The American Indians
Lost Civilizations
Mysteries of the Unknown
Time Frame
The Civil War
Cultural Atlas

COOKING
Weight Watchers® Smart Choice Recipe Collection
Great Taste~Low Fat
Williams-Sonoma Kitchen Library

SCIENCE/NATURE
Voyage Through the Universe

DO IT YOURSELF
The Time-Life Complete Gardener
Home Repair and Improvement
The Art of Woodworking
Fix It Yourself

TIME-LIFE KIDS
Library of First Questions and Answers
A Child's First Library of Learning
I Love Math
Nature Company Discoveries
Understanding Science & Nature

For information on and a full description of any of
the Time-Life Books series listed above, please call
1-800-621-7026 or write:

Reader Information
Time-Life Customer Service
P.O. Box C-32068
Richmond, Virginia 23261-2068

This volume is one in a series on world history that
uses contemporary art, artifacts, and personal accounts to
create an intimate portrait of daily life in the past.

Other volumes included in the
What Life Was Like series:

On the Banks of the Nile: Egypt, 3050-30 BC
In the Age of Chivalry: Medieval Europe, AD 800-1500
When Rome Ruled the World: The Roman Empire, 100 BC-AD 200
At the Dawn of Democracy: Classical Athens, 525-322 BC
When Longships Sailed: Vikings, AD 800-1100
Among Druids and High Kings: Celtic Ireland, AD 400-1200